D0948413

*The
Ambidextrous
Historian*

The
Ambidextrous Historian

Historical Writers
and Writing
in the American West

by
C. L. Sonnichsen

UNIVERSITY OF OKLAHOMA PRESS : NORMAN

BY C. L. SONNICHSEN

Billy King's Tombstone (Caldwell, 1942)
Roy Bean: Law West of the Pecos (New York, 1943)
Cowboys and Cattle Kings (Norman, 1950)
I'll Die Before I'll Run (New York, 1951)
Alias Billy the Kid (coauthor; Albuquerque, 1955)
Ten Texas Feuds (Albuquerque, 1957)
The Mescalero Apaches (Norman, 1958)
Tularosa: Last of the Frontier West (New York, 1960)
The El Paso Salt War (El Paso, 1961)
The Southwest in Life and Literature (New York, 1963)
Outlaw: Bill Mitchell, Alias Baldy Russell (Denver, 1964)
Pass of the North (El Paso, 1968)
The State National Bank of El Paso (coauthor; El Paso, 1971)
White Oaks, New Mexico (coauthor; Tucson, 1971)
Colonel Greene and the Copper Skyrocket (Tucson, 1974)
San Agustin: First Cathedral Church in Arizona (coauthor; Tucson, 1974)
From Hopalong to Hud (College Station, Texas, 1978)
The Grave of John Wesley Hardin (College Station, Texas, 1979)
The Ambidextrous Historian: Historical Writers and Writing in the American West
   (Norman, 1981)

Library of Congress Cataloging in Publication Data

Sonnichsen, C. L. (Charles Leland), 1901–
   The ambidextrous historian.

   Bibliography: p. 109
   Includes index.
   1. West (U.S.) – Historiography – Addresses, essays, lectures. 2. Historiography
– United States – Addresses, essays, lectures. I. Title.
F591.S67   978'.0072   81-2787
AACR2

301984

For
David and Heather,
Mason and Amy,
Shawne, Gustie,
and Matt

Contents

The
Ambidextrous
Historian

1

The Dark Night of History

An Introduction

PROFESSIONAL HISTORIANS, divided on many issues, agree on one main proposition: their discipline is sick — perhaps unto death.

To a nonprofessional, looking at the situation from the sidelines, this state of affairs is incredible and deeply disturbing. Historical studies, in his view, should be sacred and secure. The fact that we have a recorded past, he tells himself, distinguishes us from the other animals and gives us something in common with the hosts in heaven, where Saint Peter is said to keep careful records. With it, we can profit by our mistakes and become civilized. Without it, we remain as we were in the beginning — a little higher than the porpoises. History should be a cherished legacy and a joy forever, the most important subject in the curriculum. Why should Oscar Handlin of Harvard call it "a discipline in crisis"?[1]

Well, replies Handlin in his book *Truth in History*, the trouble is with the historians. They have wandered too long in Darkest Academia. "Intellectual pressures emanating from within have fragmented the discipline, loosened its cohesive elements, and worn away the consciousness of a common purpose." Historians can no longer read and write. Their careers have become "a desperate scrabbling for survival," and they have lost entirely "the unique qualifications of the trained scholar." They are overspecialized, and some of them have gone astray following such strange gods as quantification, revisionism, ethnicity, relevance, and popularity.[2]

As a consequence, the profession in the 1970's presented a sad and sorry spectacle:

It was then difficult to overestimate the spread of sheer ignorance and the deterioration of skills, as the numbers of practitioners of history had expanded in the previous decade. I do not wish to be misunderstood. I do not have in mind only the fading away of the knowledge of languages, diplomatics, paleography, and the like. Nor do I refer to the spreading darkness which hides the factual terrain outside the particular little specialty into which ever more dig themselves. I have in mind rather an ignorance more pervasive and more ominous. There were people teaching in our major universities, training other teachers, who were functionally illiterate, who simply did not know how to read or write ordinary English. Criticism in this market was deemed an unfair labor practice.[3]

"The times," Handlin concludes, "may remain hostile to the enterprise of truth. There have been such periods in the past. They [the professional historians] would do well to regard the example of those clerks in the Dark Ages who knew the worth of the task. By retiring from an alien world to a hidden monastic refuge, now and again one of them at least was able to maintain a true record."[4] In short, the best advice to a would-be historian in the latter half of the twentieth century would be Hamlet's injunction to Ophelia, slightly modified: "Get thee to a monastery. Go!"

If one tries to account for the low estate of historical studies, he may conclude that the Oscar Handlins themselves, not the times or the lower-level historians, are responsible for the situation which they deplore. Occasionally an academic historian is brave enough to admit it. Peter N. Stearns and Joel A. Tarr of Carnegie-Mellon University, for example, believe that "the discipline of history in the United States made a crucial error about forty years ago. It tragically narrowed its audience to students and other academics."[5] As the traveler in the parable fell among thieves, so the study of the past has fallen among academicians and is badly in need of a Good Samaritan. The essayists see some hope in the emergence of what they call "public history" — the examination of past experience "for such clients as unions, business and government agencies," and for "new programs, such as site preservation and the writing of family history."[6]

Handlin, of course, would never tolerate the reduction of his discipline, distressed as it is, to any such lowly-handmaid status. He proposes to make the professors even more professorial — upgrade their qualifications, remove them as far as possible from the marketplace, set them apart, make them sages and seers. The monastery, or at least the ivory tower, seems to be at the end of the road he wants to take.

Many modern academic historians, it would seem, are already far down that road. Some highly specialized scholars have left the busy world behind, communicate only with each other, and speak a private language understood only by themselves. This point was made convincingly by James Henretta of Boston University in the December, 1979, issue of the *American Historical Review* in an essay called "Social History as Lived and Written." It was a full-dress performance with critiques by two other prominent social historians, followed by a rebuttal from Henretta. Like so many of his colleagues, Henretta took a dim view of the state of his discipline: "There are many practitioners of the 'new social history' in the United States, but few theorists or philosophers."[7] Furthermore, "causal precision in the methods of quantitative research" and "analytical expertise in the theories of the social sciences" are useful tools but cannot by themselves produce first-quality history. Then, a few pages later, he adds this remarkable paragraph:

These attempts by cognitive anthropologists and phenomenologically inclined historians to comprehend the consciousness of individuals and social groups are replete with difficulty. . . . Still, important conceptual problems confront the historian who wishes to present a phenomenological portrait of a complex non-tribal society. Nonlocal or specialized institutions (such as a banking system) often cannot be depicted subjectively, because their scope extends beyond the experience of most individuals in a society. This deficiency can be offset, at least in part, by the anthropological technique of using different informants or documentary sources to construct a comprehensive picture of the social world. No individual or group sees the cultural landscape as a whole, but a mosaiclike tableau can be pieced together from the various perspectives.[8]

This passage strongly suggests that Henretta is talking in a private language, intelligible to his in-group but impenetrable to outsiders. It makes perfectly good sense—if one belongs to the club and speaks the dialect. From earliest times small elite groups have used this technique to keep vulgar outsiders from intruding on the inner circle. Some Indian tribes used a special language on the warpath. The same idea was carried out during World War II in the South Pacific when it was necessary to keep the Japanese from breaking the American codes. Navajos were employed to communicate with each other in their own language, frustrating the enemy completely. Educators speaking "Educationese" are said to puzzle the chance listener in much the same fashion. Henretta may not have aimed consciously at obfuscation, but he is obviously interested in communicating with kindred souls who share his thoughts and his vocabulary. If he is not inside the ivory tower, he is on the way up.

Handlin and Henretta, each in his own way, take an elitist view of the historian's profession, but Handlin is in a state of despair about its lower ranks and the "functional illiterates" who inhabit there. As one looks at the academic scene, he has to admit that Handlin's ideas are not without foundation, but he needs to note also that the academic historian is not the only one around. There is a whole spectrum of endeavor of which Handlin and Henretta are only dimly aware. It is peopled by men and women who know nothing of "diplomatics, paleography, and the like" and have no idea that their publications present "a phenomenological portrait of a complex, nontribal society." Their numbers—and their numbers are many—include amateurs, untrained enthusiasts, buffs, and ordinary citizens who want to know about some special corner of the past—"grassroots" types who spend long hours, happy and exciting to them, in county courthouses, old newspaper files, state archives, and regional libraries. They tape-record old-timers and correspond with living relatives of dead pioneers. They find companionship in regional historical societies and in corrals of the far-flung organization the Westerners, which has proliferated not only in the United States but in Europe and even in Japan. They publish sometimes in local and state quarterlies and in the Brand Books, Buckskin Bulletins, and Smoke Signals of their groups. They pay for publication of their pamphlets and special studies when necessary, and are convinced that all the world is waiting to hear what they have to offer. Sometimes, especially if they are outlaw-and-gunman buffs, their faith is justified.

Not all of them are either humble or obscure. There is a wide gray area between the black of the academic specialist and the white of the busy buff. State societies and special-interest groups include all sorts and conditions of men and women, from Mormon housewives interested in genealogical research to department heads in state universities. The Western History Association, a very respectable group founded by teachers of history, has room for librarians, archivists, genealogists, lost-mine and ghost-town specialists, the Council on Abandoned Military Posts, and the Westerners (who schedule an annual breakfast at the convention). Journals of the state historical societies in the West and the Brand Books of the larger corrals of the Westerners reflect this range of talent, education, and professionalism. And why not? Although Handlin seems to regard history as a plateau, it is really a ladder, and the man on the bottom rung has his place and is a member of the fraternity as well as the man on top.

Many academic historians, however—especially if they are part of the eastern establishment—give scant credit to the toilers on the lower rungs. "Builders of libraries, accumulators of documents, and publishers of source materials," Handlin feels, have done as much harm as good. "Working with old and new historical societies, they influenced many town and state histories and eased all future research." And the materials available to the local investigator have little value, in the estimation of this historian's historian. Newspapers are "ludicrous" as a source of evidence. Government documents are "particularly susceptible to misuse." Oral history is "the unverified ramblings of an eighty-year-old sharecropper, edited and arranged by unspecified standards." Although truth is the aim ("the reference point is always the evidence"), the mere collection of facts is unproductive, and the collector is hardly worthy of the true historian's notice.[9]

And yet Handlin himself states the amateur historian's creed: "What is truth? Mighty above all things, it resides in the small pieces which together form the record."[10] He might have added, "And it shall prevail," for when the buffs and amateurs, like the monks in the Dark Ages hoarding their manuscripts as they awaited a more enlightened day, have filled the archives with their documents and biographical sketches and tape recordings, the professional historian will have some, at least, of his ground prepared and seeded, and it will be easier for him to cultivate and harvest.

The reflections on history, historians, and historical writing in the western states which occupy the following pages are directed at the nonprofessional to whom history is at least a joy, and perhaps a passion. This unanointed chronicler may find in them some useful information—perhaps a better sense of his own identity and an enlarged understanding of those who share his interests. If a heavy historian should by some chance dip into them, even he may find a paragraph which will provoke debate, if not agreement.

2

The Poetry of History

MOST PEOPLE WOULD agree that poetry and history are natural opposites—as different as moonlight and money. Poetry is emotional and exciting and fanciful. History is dull and dry and factual. Poetry is poetry and history is history, and never the twain shall meet.

The truth is, they have much in common. Poetry may get along without history (though the Psalms of David and the works of Sir Walter Scott might raise a question), but history without poetry is dead, or is at least in a state of suspended animation.

To state the case properly, one needs to understand his terms. History, of course, is no problem. We all know that history is what everybody agrees to believe about any portion of the human past. Poetry is a little harder to define. To Alexander Pope it was the neat and skillful fitting of familiar ideas into metrical patterns— "what oft was thought but ne'er so well expressed."[1] Since the time of the Romantics, however, the emphasis has shifted from the mind to the heart. "Feeling is all," said Goethe, and that has been the creed of most poets ever since.[2]

Poetry starts with feeling, and feeling shapes expression in two special ways. First, under stress of feeling language begins to become rhythmical ("Darling, I love you! Will you marry me?"). In anger, love, or sorrow the accents tend to become stronger and to come with greater regularity. As a result, the language of emotion approaches the bounds of meter. Second, when our feelings are involved, we reach for metaphor. The Imagists considered a straightforward statement meaningless and insisted that only by seeing one thing in terms of another can human beings communicate. They were right, in the sense that one good image is worth a hundred words. If you tell a man his table manners are bad, he knows what you mean. But if you tell him he is a hog, he feels what you mean. And that explains why figurative language – images, metaphors, connotative or pictorial words – is the lifeblood of the poem.[3]

Everybody feels deeply about something and is therefore a potential poet. To many, perhaps most, young men, the female of the species is the most beautiful and moving of all things, though some can be found whose chief delight is a fast automobile or a good horse. For some the sight of growing things is a supreme pleasure, and a seed catalogue contains more pure poetry for them than the works of William Shakespeare. Some have a passion for the long road; some for money; some for God. For a scholar the object of all desire is a sabbatical year with a substantial grant, an important research project, and a fine library in which to complete it. These things in combination are for him what the Heavenly Jerusalem is to a saint. They bring him to the verge of poetry.

The main difference between a poet and a scholar is the poet's compulsion to communicate his feelings; the scholar is usually content to convey information. For a man to be called a poet, he has to have deeper and stronger feelings than ordinary men and a gift of expression which helps him communicate them. If he is without these gifts, he is a maker of verses and not a poet at all.

He can be a poet, of course, without writing in verse. Some of the best poetry of our century can be found in the prose works of Thomas Wolfe and William Faulkner. A selection of Wolfe's chapters has been assembled and published as poetry under the title *The Face of a Nation.*[4] Charles Dickens's famous description of the death of Little Nell, which he wrote (he said) with tears streaming down his cheeks, comes close to blank verse and has been so transcribed.[5] It would not be hard to make a case for the view that the best poems of the last seventy-five or hundred years have been written in prose and the worst of them have been written in verse.

This can all be brought home to the historian. After all, he is human too, and he has his own deep feelings. In fact, he is a historian, most probably, because he has them. He begins his career because he enjoys looking through the windows of the past. He is curious about the deeds and passions of men and women who are now dust and ashes; he loves the drums and trumpets of long ago. He is like the youth in the story of Germelshausen who finds himself in the forgotten village on the one day when the inhabitants awaken from their century-long sleep. He likes the feeling of discovery—almost of creation—as he pushes farther and farther back into Shakespeare's "dark backward and abysm of time." The towers of Babylon rise once more. The armies of Napoleon march before him. The white-topped wagons creak and strain on the Santa Fe Trail.

For a young man with this bent, a great library is the Earthly Paradise. I remember how it felt to leave the sunlight of Harvard Square every morning and enter the dim world of Widener Library. I can still smell after many years the rich, musty, faintly spicy odor of old leather bindings, and I suggest that under some circumstances book sniffing can be as enjoyable as girl watching or participating in the gusto of Schlitz. A historian, at least at the start of his studies, can feel this sort of poetry like any other man.

Many people who are not in the history business feel it too. All ancestor worshipers—genealogists, heraldry buffs, the Sons and Daughters of the American Revolution, to name a few— feel the poetry of the past. Biographers and literary antiquarians know the sensation in some degree. Even devotees of the Alley Oop comic strip are fascinated by Oop's time travels. Collectors and relic hunters of all varieties are part of the picture. If any of these things seem true or important to us—if we are capable of excitement about anything at all—to that extent we are potential poets.

The sad part of it is the tendency of these fine feelings to evaporate as the budding historian moves into his chosen path. In a few years he is likely to become dry and dull and a weariness unto student flesh. One asks oneself, Why are there so many bright young faces in the graduate seminar and so few bright old faces at the history conventions? The answer is, We get caught up in the machinery of our business. Wordsworth's ideas about childhood and maturity apply here. We come into the world, he says, "trailing clouds of glory," but with the passage of time the glory disappears. "Shades of the prison house begin to close /About the growing boy," and he "moves farther from the east."[6] Substitute "seminar" for "prison house," and the situation becomes clear.

Our training is at least partly to blame. The demand for objectivity and for precise documentation begins to squeeze out the young scholar's joy in his work and thought. His imagination must be handcuffed. He cannot make even a tiny joke or a play on words. He must avoid the first person, thus making sure that the historian is left out of history. It is as if Moses had brought down a Historian's Commandment from Mount Sinai: Be Thou Dull!

The consequences of living in this academic straitjacket begin to appear when the historian mistakes facts for truth. Truth is the sum of many facts, but in this case the whole is more than the sum of its parts. Truth is the forest, and facts are the trees which keep us from seeing it. Eugene Manlove Rhodes was commenting on this form of myopia when he remarked that it takes three facts to make a truth.[7] To approach reality, a researcher must draw some conclusions, make some deductions, think about the significance of the facts he has dug up, and that is what our education discourages us from doing. We learn that the objective historian does not make value judgments and that it is a sin to "editorialize." So we look at the trees.

Another explanation for this special sort of negative behavior is our need for security — security from criticism. We trade our freedom for it. We know what can happen to us if we are caught in an error, and anyone who has attended a historical convention and seen an established scholar make mincemeat out of a junior member of the guild knows how much blood a man can lose and still live. Hell hath no fury like an authority on military history who catches a young scholar quartering the wrong unit at Fort Bowie in 1877. Scholars may be gentle, kindly men in most of the relationships of their lives, but when they are patrolling the boundaries of their little kingdoms, they shoot trespassers first and ask questions later. Consequently the budding historian often finds himself in the position of the man in the parable who had one talent and buried it for safekeeping.

Even scholars need to remember that there is no profit without risk—that there is no real history unless a man will ask what it all adds up to, venture an opinion, throw some light on the array of facts he has assembled. He will never be Emerson's Man Thinking otherwise, and of all people the historian should be Man Thinking.[8]

Unfortunately it is the same in other disciplines as it is in history. The joy and personal rewards go out as professionalism creeps in. Shakespeare specialists get so busy counting something that they cease to enjoy Shakespeare, and Beowulf scholars, according to Tolkien's famous essay "Beowulf, the Monsters and the Critics," are in the same situation.[9]

The ironical part of it is that we richly reward a historical writer who will disregard the taboos and put the poetry back into history. We do it for Irving Stone, Bruce Catton, Samuel Eliot Morison, Arthur Schlesinger, Jr., and Bernard De Voto, to name a few. They do not prove that every student of history should think in blank verse, but they do show that the imagination need not be left out of historical writing entirely.

The question now arises, How do you get in? The problem solves itself, at least partly, if the historical writer is excited enough about what he is doing. But some concrete suggestions can be made. It comes down to this: Can you document your poetry—your metaphors, your vivid language? A conscientious historian will not invent conversations—but if he knows what was said, he can put it into direct discourse. If he can find out what kind of day it was when the Indians attacked at the Little Bighorn, he can talk about the weather. If he has been there and knows what the country looks like, he can describe it. If he knows the chief character pretty well, he can explain his feelings and motives. If he has thought about causes and consequences, he can analyze them. If he wants to communicate feeling, these are openings which he can use without violating the decencies of scholarly writing.

The twentieth century is the first to have any doubts about the role of feeling and emotion in historical writing. Our predecessors were all for it. Listen to Sir Philip Sidney's *Defense of Poesie* (1595): "... it is not ryming and versing that maketh a Poet ... but it is that fayning notable images of vertues, vices, or what els, with that delightfull teaching, which must be the right describing note to know a Poet by." The Greek historian Xenophon, he adds, "made an absolute heroicall poem" out of the *Anabasis*.[10]

About 240 years later Percy Bysshe Shelley expressed the same view in *A Defense of Poetry* (1821):

> Poets were called in the earlier epochs of the world, legislators or prophets; a poet essentially comprises and unites both these characters. For he not only beholds intensely the present as it is, but he beholds the future in the present. . . .
>
> The parts of a composition may be poetical, without the composition as a whole being a poem. . . . And thus all the great historians, Herodotus, Plutarch, Livy, were poets; although the plan of these writers, especially that of Livy, restrained them from developing this faculty in its highest degree, they made copious and ample amends for their subjection by filling the interstices of their subjects with living images.[11]

Imagine a graduate student in our time "filling the interstices of his subjects with living images"!

A little later in the nineteenth century Lord Macaulay remarked that a historian should ideally be a combination of *poet* and *philosopher*.[12] We can go partway with him, for we award the highest historical standing to philosophers of history: Oswald Spengler, Arnold Toynbee, W. H. McNeill, Vilfredo Pareto, and a handful of others. The poet-historian makes his way in our time with a little more difficulty, but he is with us too, and not without honor. He is the rare writer who has the feeling and the power of lan-

guage to convey to us his vision of truth. Take the beginning of
Arthur Schlesinger's *The Age of Jackson:*

> For the White House the new year began in gloom. The Presi-
> dent's wife spent a sleepless and painful night, and Mr. Adams,
> waking at daybreak, found the dawn overcast, the skies heavy and
> sullen. He prayed briefly, then fumbled for his Bible and turned to
> the Book of Psalms, reading slowly by the yellow light of his shaded
> oil lamp. "Blessed *is* the man that walketh not in the counsel of the
> ungodly, nor standeth in the way of sinners, nor sitteth in the seat of
> the scornful." On he read to the ultimate assurance. "For the Lord
> knoweth the way of the righteous: but the way of the ungodly shall
> perish."
>
> The familiar words assuaged the disappointments of four years.
> To an Adams, the first psalm seemed almost a personal pledge.
> "It affirms that the righteous man is, and promises that he shall be,
> blessed," he noted with precise gratification in his journal, and went
> to his desk for his usual early-morning work. As his pen began to
> scratch across the paper, the lamp, its oil low, flared for a moment,
> then flickered out. Mr. Adams sat in the gray light (J. Q. Adams,
> *Memoirs,* VIII, 89).[13]

The passage sounds fictionized, but Schlesinger has been at
pains to substantiate every detail. What he contributes from his
own stock-in-trade is evocative language — words which convey
feeling as well as meaning; adjectives and verbs which paint
pictures. The skies are not just gray; they are "heavy and sullen."
Adams "fumbles" for his Bible. He reads by "the yellow light of his
shaded oil lamp." When he writes, his pen begins "to scratch
across the paper." This is legitimate use of the imagination and it is
open to every writer of history outside the graduate school. It
follows the same road as the newspaperman's commandment:
"Show me; don't tell me!"

Schlesinger makes Jackson a believable human being, commenting
on his "natural grandeur which few men could resist" — his "grim,
majestic visage" — his "calculated rages." He makes him real by
introducing little vignettes from Jessie Benton Frémont's mem-
oirs:

15

Jessie Benton knew she must keep still and not fidget or squirm, even when General Jackson twisted his fingers too tightly in her curls. The old man, who loved children, liked to have Benton bring his enchanting daughter to the White House. Jessie, clinging to her father's hand, trying to match his strides, would climb breathlessly up the long stairs to the upper room where, in the sunshine flooding in through the tall south windows, they would find the General in his big rocking chair close to the roaring wood fire. The child instinctively responded to the lonely old man's desire for "a bright, unconscious affectionate little life near him," and would sit by his side while his hand rested on her head. Sometimes, in the heat of discussion, his long, bony fingers took a grip that made Jessie look at her father but give no other sign.[14]

Such passages are appetizers. The bulk of the book is solid, meat-and-potatoes fact. But Schlesinger has his vision and he speaks from his heart. He knows what the Age of Jackson was and how it fits into the pattern of our history. He loves it and understands it and wants his reader to love and understand it too. His enthusiasm generates a language and a method which make communication possible. He writes history; he does not get lost in the facts. He is aware of something which many Americans saw once but few see now. Emerson saw it in 1884 and wrote it into an essay called, significantly for the purpose of this chapter, "The Poet":

> We have yet had no genius in America, with tyrannous eye, which knew the value of our incomparable materials, and saw, in the barbarism and materialism of the times, another carnival of the same gods whose picture he so much admires in Homer; then in the Middle Age; then in Calvinism. Banks, and tariffs, the newspaper and caucus, Methodism and Unitarianism, are flat and dull to dull people, but rest on the same foundations of wonder as the town of Troy and the temple of Delphi, and are as swiftly passing away. Our log-rolling, our stumps and their politics, our fisheries, our Negroes and Indians, our boasts and our repudiations, the wrath of rogues and the pusillanimity of honest men, the northern trade, the Southern planting, the western clearing, Oregon and Texas, are yet unsung. Yet America is a poem in our eyes: its ample geography dazzles the imagination, and it will not wait long for metres.[15]

Professional historians need to remember — and to teach — that bricks alone do not make a building. An architect is needed to make something out of the bricks. Someone is needed to assemble the facts according to his design, to try to understand what they mean. Most historical writers have to be content with making contributions to history, but some can be historians. For these chosen few, history is as much feeling as fact, and they can pass the feeling on to others. They can teach the rest of us to enjoy history and not be ashamed of our reactions. They resemble Sir Philip Sidney trying to find a way to say what he felt: "Foole," said my Muse to me, "Looke in thy heart and write."[16]

You will note that Sidney's muse did not say, "Look in thy Turabian." The Muse of History does not say such a thing either. What she does say to those who stop to listen is: "Call no man historian unless he makes you feel."

3

The Ambidextrous Historian

HAPPINESS IS an individual matter. For a child a warm puppy may be the answer. For a young man it may be a matter of sex. For an old man it is said to involve successful elimination. For a historian of the academic variety it is publication in a first-class journal. Publication oils the wheels of his public and private life. Promotion and salary depend on it. Nothing good can happen to him unless he has published. There is, however, one unwritten proviso—he must stay in his "discipline."

Laymen cannot appreciate the strength of this taboo, but the halls of Academe are strewn with the bodies of those who left the beaten path. I cite the example of a man who was for a number of years the state historian of a large and important western commonwealth. During his tenure he published or edited some thirty books, all bearing on the history of his state. Then, for good and sufficient reasons, he abandoned his specialty, earned a Ph.D. in English, and became a professor in a state university. When he applied for membership in the graduate faculty, however, the screening committee refused to recommend him in spite of the length of his bibliography. His publications, they said, were "not in his discipline."

This man is by no means an isolated example. Colleges and universities provide new illustrations every year of the bad effects of a narrowly disciplinary approach to the pursuit of truth. When the Ph.D. in American Studies was thought up at Harvard a few generations ago, it seemed like an excellent idea. What could be more productive than a cross-disciplinary consideration of thought and action in the United States through its history and literature? The difficulty was that the products of the program were in limbo when they finished. When the time came to look for a job, they had to choose between American history and American literature because the departments were set up that way.

Sometimes a nonconformist jumps the fence, and he is the subject of this essay. There is no name for him as yet, but he could be called a "poor wayfaring scholar," like the poor wayfaring stranger in the old hymn. And like the boll weevil in another song, he is "jest lookin' fer a home." He doesn't belong anywhere.

It is unnecessary to feel sorry for him, however. He is fortunate in his freedom and makes his contribution because he *is* free, offering a modest example to those who would avoid disciplinary paralysis. Historians, of all scholars, need the lesson. If he is to do his job well, the historian needs to know something about anthropology, sociology, economics, political science, philosophy, literature, and a great many other specialties—at least, the more he knows about some or all of these subjects, the better his equipment. Department heads and deans and graduate faculties agree that this is the truth, but they do not do anything about it. The poor wayfaring scholar has to do it on his own. He must settle for less and less knowledge about more and more areas while his colleagues are striving to learn more and more about less and less—until they know everything about nothing.

Already they find it impossible to see the forest. They see only the trees and sometimes only a branch or a leaf as their specialties grow narrower and narrower and the field of history grows broader and broader. A few decades ago historians wrote for the public. Then they began writing for each other. Now they write for their fellow specialists—a fact which accounts for the desiccation of scholarly journals. Who reads the two top American historical quarterlies? The answer is, Nobody *reads* them. Perhaps one scholar in ten consults the one article which deals with his subspecialty because it will help him write an article of his own. So what is done with the top historical quarterlies? They are filed. If they are lucky, they are taken off the shelf once every ten years for dusting.

Some truths can be learned only by cutting across the disciplines. Any outside knowledge or experience gives depth and breadth. Lawyers and engineers bring a wider perspective to business. Doctors can and do add to our information about music and literature. Every specialist needs a background in something besides his specialty so that he can see it from the outside. If he is not ambidextrous, he ought to be.

Savoie Lottinville points out in *The Rhetoric of History* that in Europe it is almost a rule that a great historical scholar comes into his field from some other area. Leopold von Ranke was a philologist. Henry Buckle was a linguist who knew nineteen languages. In our own country Francis Parkman was an outdoorsman who had nonhistorical reasons for investigating the Oregon Trail. John Motley was a lawyer, novelist, and diplomat. Lottinville recommends that all historians should be trained in "rhetoric," which he defines as "the honest stratagems as old as Xenophon's trick of putting first things first," and that they should learn to employ "all of the devices that have been created since the Assyrians, Babylonians, Greeks, and the Western world's Maya authors committed their heroic and religious accounts and poetry to writing."[1]

In short, What does he know of history who only history knows?

To come down to specifics, I should like to spotlight two outside disciplines which are especially useful to a historian: folklore and popular culture. He deals with them whether he knows it or not, but he uses them better if he knows what he is doing.

They are really two sides of the same thing: the assumptions—the things taken for granted—by which people live and the patterns of conduct which result from these assumptions. The difference is that folklore is *then* and popular culture is *now*. Folklore studies the traditional; popular culture studies the contemporary. Anything we say or think or do because we say or think or do it is the raw material of both, and folklorists are becoming more and more aware that high-school slang is just as much folklore as mountaineer talk in the Blue Ridge Mountains.

It is natural, of course, for students of the past to deal first of all with traditional folklore—the assumptions we used to live by—and they are an important part of the record. In frontier times, particularly in Texas, many people considered revenge a duty. The idea that a man should right his own wrongs was accepted without question or examination, and many Texans were buried as a result. The idea of manifest destiny, accepted uncritically among nineteenth-century Americans, was influential in the expansion of the United States to the Pacific. The Jews likewise thought it was God's will that they should occupy the Promised Land, even though it belonged to somebody else at the time. The familiars of the Spanish Inquisition had their special assumptions, just as the Weathermen did a few centuries later. A historian cannot understand Andrew Jackson unless he knows something about the way people thought in Tennessee when Andrew was growing up. Today's assumptions, one might say, are tomorrow's history. What people take for granted makes history as well as horse races.

A thousand examples of unreflective behavior are at hand. When you are strolling with a lady, you take the outside of the walk. Once you did it to shelter her from flying mud on the street side and from spattering slops from above. Now you do it because that is the way it is done. An Englishman keeps his fork in his left hand and piles his mashed potatoes on the back. He thinks you are a barbarian because you switch the implement to your right hand, after cutting your meat, and use it as a shovel. In the Orient, some people say, you express approval of your meal by belching vigorously. In America a belch will get you thrown out. Charles Dickens lost face in Boston on his first visit to the United States because he combed his hair at the dinner table, but he himself was upset by the Americans' penchant for spittoons (though he was impressed by the accuracy and precision of their spitting).[2]

Look at the subject this way—and I believe it is the right way—and you find folklore and history working together in the most unexpected places. I call attention to this vignette by Robert Pilpel from the Wrap-around section of *Harper's* magazine for January, 1975:

> I finally managed to track down Big B. Wolf (his friends refer to him affectionately as "The") at Queens College, where he is a gradu-

ate student in sociology. At first he was extremely reluctant to discuss his part in the Three Little Pigs incident. "Why rake over the past?" he said. "I'm a totally different person now. I have a much better understanding of my needs." I pressed him, however, to provide some insight into his formerly antisocial behavior.

"To begin with," he said, relenting, "a wolf's role in today's society is so incredibly ambivalent it's a wonder any of us ever make a satisfactory adjustment. I mean, on the one hand, we're supposed to be solitary and promiscuous — the old 'lone wolf' stereotype — and on the other hand we're supposed to run with a pack and conform."

How had this role ambivalence affected him personally?

"Well," he said, wiping away some of the saliva that kept accumulating around his chops, "my father felt these conflicting role demands very strongly, and they made it very difficult for him to relate to me in any meaningful way. I think he may even have resented me a little."

"Did that have anything to do with your run-in with the pigs?"

"Oh, definitely. I had just moved away from home for the first time, see, and I went through a sort of identity crisis. I was feeling very lonely and insecure."

So when he tried to relate to the three little pigs and they rejected him, he blew their house in. They called the police, and he was "institutionalized." Now he has been in analysis for a couple of years and has recently got engaged: ". . . together we walked to the library where a pretty young girl with a basket and a red cloak was waiting."[3]

Think what a folklorist-historian by my definition could do with this! It is fairly crawling with the kinds of assumptions that are so familiar to us that we do not even think of them as assumptions. You can see them for yourself, and I will pause only long enough to suggest that Pilpel's piece is a commentary on Original Sin. We can all admit now without irreverence that Original Sin is part of the folklore of our ancestors. It was their way of explaining the perversity of the human animal. Substitute "adjustment" for "grace," and it becomes obvious that Pilpel is pointing out the formulas — the assumptions — by which *we* explain the perversities of the human animal. The introduction of Father Wolf makes the sin (antisocial behavior) "original."

The main difference between John Calvin's formula and Pilpel's is that Calvin was *then* and Pilpel is *now*. *Then* is folklore. *Now* is popular culture. Four centuries ago Original Sin was popular culture. Four centuries from now psychiatry may well be folklore. A historian needs to be aware of these things. He needs to be ambidextrous.

On my desk lies the summer, 1974, issue of the *Journal of Popular Culture*. I note an article by Ronny E. Turner and Charles K. Edgley called "'The Devil Made Me Do It!' Popular Culture and Religious Vocabularies of Motive."[4] It would seem that Original Sin may sometimes be *now*, and may even be popular culture.

A few pages farther on, the magazine carries a discussion of the craze for fins and bright-metal decoration on motor cars of the 1950s. It is called "Orgasm in Chrome."[5] A historian, and perhaps even a student of traditional folklore, might be taken aback by such a title and leave the field to the popular-culturists, but there is no doubt that fins can be folklore, if we wait long enough, and part of the history of American transportation.

One important difference between folklorist and popular-culturist needs to be pointed out. The latter operates at the end of a shorter rope. He is trapped in the *now* and the *popular,* just as the folklorist is usually trapped in the *then* and the *provincial.* The poor wayfaring scholar, however, is not trapped at all. He moves freely across boundaries and deals with any aspect of his material. He does not have to get out of the way for anyone — not for the psychologists or the sociologists or the anthropologists or the folklorists or the popular-culturists. He can see the whole picture better than any of them. Let me show you how it works.

For the last ten years or so I have made a speciality of the fiction about the Indian wars in the Southwest — the Apache campaigns. I study it as social or intellectual history, and some very interesting facts have emerged. Remembering that we live in an era when the whole nation seems to be suffering from guilt pangs about what we have done to our red brothers (ignoring what our red brothers have done to us), we are startled to find that on the popular (mostly paperback) level our basic assumptions have not changed much since the days of the dime novel. The Apache is still a subhuman, larcenous, lecherous, murderous, repulsive creature. He resembles Grendel the Moorstalker. He is ruthless and unclean, incredibly cruel, exhibiting fiendish ingenuity in devising tortures for his captives. A white woman suffers the tortures of the damned if she falls into his hands. He flaunts all of the offensive traits and habits that we, as "civilized" people, try studiously to avoid. In short, he is not just an enemy. He is The Enemy, a product of our inherited and instinctive fears and revulsions. He belongs in the realm of folklore. As evidence I quote from an article of mine entitled "The Ambivalent Apache" in the August, 1975, issue of the quarterly magazine of the Western Literature Association:

> It goes without saying that The Enemy must be totally bad. No redeeming features are possible. And if he is not bad enough to suit us, we work on him until he is. The way we go about it is clear from even a casual look at the Apache in popular fiction.
> First of all, he is filthy in his habits and he smells bad. He has a "rank, feral breath" (Don Catlin, *Desert Crucible*, 1965) and gives off "a potent smell of sweat and grease and smoke and bird lime and the Lord knew what all" (Hal G. Evarts, *The Blazing Land*, 1960, 1966). The Apache warrior is "filthy in his ideas and speech and inconceivably dirty in his person and manners" (James Warner Bellah, *A Thunder of Drums*, 1961). This sometimes goes for the women as well as for the men: "Apache women's habits leave them offensive and even in the earlier years, few mountain men wanted one for a wife" (Will Cook, *Apache Ambush*, 1955, 1960). A sensitive nose could pick up the Apache odor even at a distance:
>
> "What's the matter, boy?" Hardhead said.
> Billy whispered, "Apaches, Pa. I smell 'em." (Harry Whittington, *Desert Stakeout*, 1961)
>
> It should be no surprise to a generation pathologically sensitive to human body odors that the Apache should offend in this way. Our consumption of deodorants (roll on, spray on, pat on, rub on), mouthwashes and aids to "feminine daintiness" makes the point. Since we must at best smell good and at worst not smell at all, The Enemy could not smell any way but bad.[6]

Anthropologists say that Indians do not really smell bad at all. They just smell different. And if one of them burns mesquite in his tipi or hogan or wickiup, he smells different from one who burns piñon. Here, however, as in other departments of human affairs, to be different is to be offensive.

A popular-culturist might very well stop here and consider his job done. He would not see any point in checking the Apache out in the upper crust of western novels, mostly hardback, with some pretensions to consideration as "literature." That would take him out of his area of interest—what we once called his "discipline." But by staying in his field he misses half of the truth about the ambivalent Apache—in some ways the more interesting half. He would be astonished at what he would find, so to speak, on the other side of the tracks. There the whole traditional set of assumptions about the Apache—and about the Indian in general—have been turned upside down. The savage is now the white man.

Sympathy for the Indian, with heavy condemnation for the frontiersman, goes back a long way in American fiction. Ever since Helen Hunt Jackson's *Ramona* (1884) and Adolph Bandelier's *The Delight Makers* (1890), increasing numbers of serious novelists have taken the side of the native American and blamed all the scalping and burning and torturing on the white man. In the 1940s the movement went all the way, and it has been snowballing ever since. Elliott Arnold's *Blood Brother* (1947) made the Apaches just a little lower than the angels—a fine, sensitive, religious group of people, in tune with nature and with each other—much superior to the whites who were lying to them and cheating them and harrying them. Fourteen years later Jane Barry's *A Time in the Sun* pushed the trend about as far as it would go. Anna, the heroine, is a white girl who is captured by Apaches in Arizona as she is on her way to join her soldier-fiancé. She falls in love with one of her captors, half Apache and half Mexican, named Joaquín, and marries him. The question of who is scalping whom comes up between them:

> "They burned a man. Burned him!"
> He said, "Have you ever seen Apache scalps on Mexican and American saddles? Have you seen them geld and flay our wounded? Or what they do to our dead if we don't recover them?" [7]

There it is! The Apaches are the good guys; the white men are the villains. They are doing what Indians were once supposed to make a business of doing. Most intelligent readers in our time have been conditioned to believe that in many ways the Apache was superior to his conqueror and that the real atrocities were visited on the red man by the white. The bookstores are overflowing with "Indian" books, and they are all more or less starry-eyed about Indian life and character. They tell us that Custer died for your sins and that the Indian knows how to touch the earth — that this land was theirs and we ought to give it back to them. I doubt that anyone could get a book published if he did not climb up on this bandwagon or tried to upset it. Only in the paperback novels are the old assumptions tolerated, and even there one finds the new assumptions creeping in.

It is obvious that the consumers of popular westerns cherish a set of assumptions completely opposite from those of more sophisticated readers. If either side has its doubts, they do not often come to the surface, for the Apache continues to be ambivalent in novel after novel year after year. And unless one is willing to take all folklore and popular history to be his province, he will not really know what is going on.

Here, as is easily seen, the poor wayfaring scholar — the ambidextrous historian — makes his entry. He has no fixed academic home and is not obliged to stay in his discipline. He can cover the entire range of subject matter as other scholars could hardly do. His homelessness gives him a very special advantage.

One might say that scholars are like a group of Indians sitting around a kettle of stew. Everybody is interested in the contents, which is dog meat, but each one reaches for whatever portion he finds most interesting. Our scholars in the same fashion are concerned with human behavior, but each one chooses a different portion. Archaeologists are interested in artifacts. Folklorists and popular-culturists are interested in what Joseph Arpad calls "mentifacts," for which my term is "assumptions."[8] The ambidextrous wayfaring scholar is curious about both, and about many other things too.

He makes the choice, which all human beings must make, between freedom and security. There is much to be said for putting your money in a good, sound savings account at 5 percent. There is also much to be said for buying stocks and hoping for bigger returns. One man chooses to stay comfortably with a wife he knows too well. Another takes off with a chorus girl whom he does not know at all. The wayfaring scholar has chosen the chorus girl. He is free. He can deal with conventional folklore or with popular culture. He can shift from *then* to *now*, from the provincial to the literary, from the fantastic to the serious. He has taken the whole range of human assumptions to be his province, and he is not really looking for a home. He would be uncomfortable in it if he had one.

4

Caveat Scriptor

The Regional Historian and His Publishers

WHEN THE NINETEENTH-CENTURY American novelist Hamlin Garland found himself in the company of a stranger and felt it necessary to start a conversation, he would smile graciously and inquire, "Well, how's the book coming?"

Almost invariably the stranger would register shock and ask, "How did you know?"

It is the same today. Everybody is writing, has written, or is thinking about writing something. One wonders why. Writing is a highly specialized and highly competitive business. It requires unusual talents and considerable preparation. A man needs to produce a million words, the experts say, before he is fit to publish. J. Frank Dobie once remarked that it takes ten years to write a good book. Many a writer, including this one, has struggled for seven years to achieve print. And yet thousands of otherwise perceptive and intelligent people dream of writing a successful book the first time around and becoming rich and famous overnight. This typical query came from a friend in Dallas in the summer of 1978: "My future continues to be more uncertain than usual. What do you think of my chances to write a book? I know nothing of the book market except that I buy too many. What kind of book sells best, or at least can get published?"

This very bright woman would never have announced, "I am about to become a professional woman golfer and go on the tour." She would never have considered seeking employment in a beauty parlor without some training. Why should she expect to compete successfully with professionals in what is coming to be—next to snake charming and marriage—the world's most difficult business? She is only one of many, however, and some of them are western historians.

The writing bug bites them for several reasons. If they are in academic life, they have to publish. If they are amateurs, they want to publish because they have something to say that seems to them important. The parable of the man who buried his one talent is in the back of their minds. Buried and hidden, their information does no one any good, and so they say to themselves, "People will surely want to know about this."

Their absorbing interest, sometimes amounting to obsession, pushes them a little farther down the road. Just as a hen thinks that eggs must be the primary interest of all living things, so the tireless researcher who knows all about buttons on Confederate uniforms or Lieutenant Beale's road across northern Arizona is convinced that the world is waiting for his conclusions and that a major publisher in the East will share his enthusiasm.

He has to be wrong, of course, and his book has about as much chance in New York as a snowball in Phoenix. Once he is convinced of this painful fact, he may be ready to listen to advice about the resources that are open to him. The question is, how does one convince him?

One is tempted to begin as Bob Hope is said to have begun when he was called on to make a commencement speech to a group of college seniors. "You are about to go out into the world to take up its burdens and solve its problems," he said. "My advice to you is, 'Don't go!'"

The advice is good. This is the worst of all times for an unknown writer to attempt to interest a commercial publisher. It can happen, but it almost never does. For one thing, the business is too big. Trying to get aboard is like attempting to get on a 747 in full flight.

The preliminary "Annual Summary" printed by *Publishers Weekly* in its issue of February 22, 1980, reveals that 37,222 new and reissued book titles were published in 1979. This divides out into almost 120 a day. How many manuscripts did not make it? How many were rejected and sent back? How many were not even read? There is no way of knowing. "A hundred sent to one accepted," I guessed in the presence of August Lenniger of the New York agency. "A thousand to one!" he replied indignantly.

Any publisher will tell you that he is swamped with submissions, some by competent people, more by first-timers who are innocent of knowledge about bookmaking. Every major United States publishing house is said to receive about five thousand manuscripts every year "over the transom" – that is, without invitation or query.[1] The word is out that most of the big firms have abolished the "slush pile" – the heap of unsolicited manuscripts – and that they will return your book unread if you have enclosed a stamped, self-addressed envelope. If you have neglected this formality, your supreme effort goes into the shredder.

In 1975, Chuck Ross decided to find out just how much attention the orphan manuscript gets. He sent off another man's prize-winning novel, with a good record of sales, to fourteen publishers, including the one which had issued it. Every one of them turned it down; not a one recognized it for what it was. The next step was to try it on forty-six literary agents. Only one was interested, and he wanted twenty-five dollars to read it.[2]

University presses are as badly overloaded and as unreceptive as the commercial houses. As labor and production costs go up and manuscripts come storming in, the director is likely to awaken some morning and find himself overcommitted. Only a few years ago, the biggest of the western university presses, which had been turning out a book a week, had to cut back on production. It would be three years before some accepted manuscripts could be scheduled. An editor for this press told me that many were being returned to the authors with an explanation and the suggestion that they try another publisher.[3] At least two important university presses in 1978 would not even look at a potentially publishable book. There was just no room at the inn. The book they would not look at was one of mine.

Placing a magazine article is almost as hard. Periodical publishers, as well as book publishers, seem more and more inclined to turn to staff writers or to outsiders commissioned to do a particular job. Rex Alan Smith's book on the Wounded Knee "massacre" was done under contract for *Reader's Digest* and issued in 1975 under the title *Moon of Popping Trees.* In the same year, on another front, a western writer sent an essay to *American Heritage* telling about a Revolutionary Pennsylvania militiaman who campaigned against Indians in Ohio in 1777 and 1778. He burned their cornfields, and they nearly burned him at the stake. Neither side could have guessed that two centuries later the white man's descendants would consider the Indians in the right and Jonathan Gillam in the wrong. The editor sent the piece back with a kind letter explaining that he had already engaged another writer to do a "similar piece."[4] The rejected essay stayed in circulation and was eventually published in the Cowboy Hall of Fame's *Persimmon Hill,*[5] won a Golden Spur from Western Writers of America, and was printed in their 1977 *Spurs* anthology.[6] The author was lucky. I appreciate his luck because I was the author. Obviously the staff writer is making it harder and harder for the free-lancer to get published.

In such a situation competition among authors is bound to be intense. Only the best qualified or best known have a chance with a major publisher. Only the most commercially promising manuscripts are in the running. It is not enough that you speak or write the language well. You have to be exceptionally good at it. It is not enough that your research has been thorough and that all your facts are straight. Your subject has to be interesting to casual readers. It is not enough that you make your points clearly and cogently. You have to know how to arouse interest, appeal to the imagination, and even create suspense. As Savoie Lottinville points out in *The Rhetoric of History* (distilled from his thirty years of experience as head of the University of Oklahoma Press), the age-old rules of good composition apply to historical writing as well as to other kinds.[7] Unless the would-be historian knows something about them, he will remain anonymous.

Another obstacle to be surmounted as the western historian

tries for type is the provincialism of eastern editors and publishers. Even the ones who publish western books believe in their hearts that no one west of the Mississippi can read. Vine Deloria summed up the situation with some bitterness in an interview printed in *Suntracks IV* (1978), published at the University of Arizona:

> In order to get a book published, the publisher has to be convinced that it is a commercial book. What that means in the minds of most editors is that it will sell in New York City. And New York City sells one quarter of the books that are sold in this country every year. Maybe a best-selling book will never reach the West—very few copies will reach the West—but if it sells in the bookstores in New York then it is a best seller. So you have a problem of being out West whether you're an Indian or any other kind of writer if you're out of the New York area. New Yorkers are basically stupid. They really don't believe there is anything west of the Hudson. There may be a few trees and rocks, but outside of that, there's nothing, see? So readers can start from a Western perspective and assume that your readers know certain things. When the manuscript gets to New York and those editors look at it, then they change the whole thing around. So that you're communicating with the people who live in that string from Boston to Washington . . . you end up not knowing who you are writing for. . . . And you can't ever crack that.[8]

The one word which stands out in Deloria's Jeremiad is "commercial." The big publishers have to make money, lots of money, especially since so many of them have been taken over by conglomerate corporations whose executives see no difference between a book and a bar of soap. Most of the time they are right in assuming that a western book will not go in "the string from Boston to Washington." They will gamble, but not on a dark horse. Sometimes they miss a good thing as a result—like Carobeth Laird's *Encounter with an Angry God* (1975), which was printed by a small institutional press on a California Indian reservation.[9] But they are experts in judging public taste and predicting what will sell, and probably they hit oftener than they miss.

A number of the big houses (such as Houghton Mifflin; Little, Brown; Oxford University Press) make a subspecialty of western books and present a brave show of looking for good new western authors. For years Alfred A. Knopf and Angus Cameron, his second-in-command (now retired) attended the annual conventions of the Western History Association and cultivated the acquaintance of the members. They seldom found the sort of writer they were looking for, however, and regional specialists who felt encouraged to submit manuscripts were often (perhaps usually) tactfully turned down. Cameron used two standard gambits in explaining the rejections. "Your book is written down, not written," he would say. Sometimes he summed it all up in one word: "Monographic."

As I understand it, this means that the manuscript under discussion is a recital of facts and lacks imagination. It might be studied, but it would not be read. It might also need improvement in structure, characterization, narrative method, and word sense, but these considerations would only be aspects of the central problem. Angus considered it a pedestrian performance; it did not take off; it had no emotional appeal; it would not create its own interest; it would not make money.

Is this legitimate criticism? Does a historical work need to read like a novel? If it does have this kind of charm, is it not "popular" rather than "scholarly" and therefore second-rate? The historians who teach in the universities and train the next generation of scholars seem to be of two minds about this. They all agree that what the history business needs most is good writing, but the work they accept from graduate students is always "monographic" and usually "written down, not written." If one of those students manages to develop a style and finds a way of reaching a nonacademic audience, he does it on his own.

One man probably set the standard for Knopf and Cameron. They were both deeply impressed by Bernard De Voto (see Wallace Stegner's *The Uneasy Chair*),[10] and one suspects that their western pilgrimages were made in the hope that De Voto would rise again. Bennie did not rise, of course. There will never be another *Across the Wide Missouri*, but hope sprang eternal in their breasts, and probably also in the breasts of Sheldon Meyer, of Oxford; Ned Bradford, of Little, Brown; and all the other editors who were convinced that American books, western or eastern, have to sell in "the strip between Boston and Washington" if they are going to sell at all.

These facts should be kept in mind by the western historian who has illusions about interesting an eastern publisher. He should ask himself, "Will anyone in Connecticut want to read this book?" If the answer is negative, he will save time and trouble for busy editors and for himself if he looks elsewhere for a publisher.

On the other hand, if he has worked hard and long, the difficulty of breaching the eastern market is no excuse for hanging up his spurs and leaving the battle. Up to this point the emphasis has been on the difficulty—the near impossibility—of interesting a major eastern house in publishing a western regional book. The advice offered has been, "*Caveat Scriptor*—Let the Writer Beware." There is, however, a brighter side. The regional historian is not without recourse if he once makes up his mind that it is useless to try to storm the heavens where the successors of Knopf and Cameron sit enthroned. He can leave his modest legacy to posterity and enjoy the supreme thrill of passing out autographed copies of his work to his colleagues and his relatives. The secret is to look for publishing possibilities close at hand.

For really superior work a university press may be the answer. Most of them insist on detailed documentation, which means that, unlike Angus Cameron, they *want* the book to be "monographic." Some bilious critics maintain that a university press will not look at a book unless it is dull and lifeless—that is, scholarly—but those of us who have worked with university presses know that this is not true. Some subjects, technical, scientific, statistical, cannot possibly be made lively and imaginative. To fashion an inspirational and creative document out of *Late Quaternary Mollusks of the Rio Grande Valley* (by Artie L. Metcalf [El Paso: Texas Western Press, 1967]) would be impossible, and the attempt would be ridiculous. But history and biography can and should touch the imagination, and directors of university presses are as excited as any New York editor about a fine piece of writing, limited though the subject may be.

In still another respect the university-press man resembles the editor in New York. He is not obliged to make money, but he does have to break even. His books must find buyers and readers, or he operates in the red, runs out of storage space for his unsold volumes, and is investigated and probably fired by the publications committee or the board of regents. There is no place in his program for books of very limited appeal.

Should an author, for this or any other reason, have no luck with the university presses, he has a number of options still open to him. One is the subsidy press. This is not the same as a vanity press, which will publish anything for money. A press which accepts a subsidy calculates the risk and decides that it can publish your book and remain solvent if you help with the expenses. Usually you do not have to assume the whole burden, as with a vanity press, and you get royalties — perhaps enough to cover your outlay. You share the risk with the publisher.

Subsidy publishing has been with us for a long time and is becoming more and more common. Scholars in the sciences are used to paying for the publication of their articles, on which prestige and promotion depend, and they do not feel insulted if a publisher calls for help in issuing a book or monograph of limited appeal. University presses have been known to use a financial crutch, though the practice has not been common or necessary because of the state or institutional funds set aside to keep the press in operation. One academic press that I know of agreed to print a book of purely local interest in return for a $10,000 subsidy, which it disguised as the source of an annual "best book" prize. Even New York publishers may stand with palm extended, and many regional writers, myself included, know this from first-hand experience.

In this connection, some special situations may arise which can catch a local chronicler off guard. One Arizona publisher with whom I was acquainted offered a standard contract with normal royalties, but was said to find himself in difficulties when the book was in press. Costs had gone up. Unexpected outlays had depleted his funds. There would be a long wait before publication — unless the author wanted to share the expense. The author usually did.

Professional or near-professional writers, including those who produce popular history, pretend to be untouched by such sordid matters as subsidies and shared expenses. "I would not even begin a book without a contract and a healthy advance on royalties," your old-pro friend will tell you. He is forgetting that once he too was struggling to interest a publisher—any publisher. You, of course, are not a professional, and your troubles are just beginning. You may have to pay to play.

There are, however, several ways to spend your money. There is self-publishing, for instance. This involves finding a printer who is able and willing to design an attractive volume. He will compute costs of designing, printing, lithographing, correcting proofs, and binding. You will pay him for his work, pick up your 500 or 1,000 copies, and sell them yourself.

It can be done successfully. In 1975, Helen Baldock Craig published *Within Adobe Walls*,[11] the story of her life on a historic Arizona ranch. She organized a one-woman bookselling campaign, visiting bookstores, telling friends, placing reviews in newspapers, making talks. In two and a half months, she says, she made 100 public appearances and sold 2,000 copies of her product. Similar experiences are reported by many others. "It isn't so awfully difficult to publish your own book," says the editor of the New Mexico Book League's *Book Talk*. "It is much like a recipe for a rather fancy dish. Follow the directions carefully and success will be yours. At last count there are over 125 self-publishers (individuals) in New Mexico."[12]

Plenty of help is at hand for the beginner. *Words into Type*, by Marjorie E. Skillin and Robert M. Gay, is a good book to start with,[13] and a dozen handbooks are available. Bill Henderson's *The Publish-It-Yourself Handbook: Literary Tradition and How-To* tells how self-publishing has worked for various authors. Other titles, useful in different ways, include Dan Poynter's *The Self-Publishing Manual; Publish It Yourself*, by Charles J. Chickadel; and *The Encyclopedia of Self-Publishing*, by Marilyn and Tom Moss.[14] So much interest has been aroused that a trade magazine seemed called for, and between 1972 and 1975 Sibley S. Morrill of San Francisco published *The Self Publishing Writer*. Until he died in 1975, Morrill served a growing number of do-it-yourselfers. Even *Publishers Weekly* has discussed the phenomenon.[15]

We continue to hear of new developments. One is the proliferation of new imprints. Frequently an ambitious or prolific writer will start his own. In effect, he is a self-publisher, but a press name on his title page adds a little extra standing: Prickly Pear Press, Lonesome Buffalo Press, Hungry House. In time he may be the owner of a bonafide publishing business. Ghost-town and mining-camp specialist Stanley Paher of Las Vegas, Nevada, founded Nevada Publications some years ago, and his books (for example, *Colorado River Ghost Towns*, 1976) appear with almost alarming frequency. Frank Mangan, with experience as editor of a trade magazine, set up The Press/El Paso in his home town and published *El Paso in Pictures* in 1971. Later he changed the name to Mangan Books and began publishing other authors. Winter Griffith, a Tucson doctor, decided to write a series of handbooks for physicians when heart problems forced his retirement from the faculty of the University of Arizona Medical School in 1979. He registered as a publisher with the state corporation commission; paid fifty dollars to rent a post-office box; subcontracted his typesetting, printing, and binding; and was on his way as an educational publisher.[16]

If self-publishing seems to involve too much time, trouble, and money, it is often possible to find a small publisher who is looking for a special kind of manuscript. Jim Earle, a faculty member at Texas A&M University, got his Creative Press under way in 1978 with the publication of Chuck Parsons's *The Capture of John Wesley Hardin*.[17] The obvious problem, of course, is to find the small press that is counting the hours until your manuscript arrives. You may find it listed in the telephone directory of the city nearest you. The Tucson directory in 1980 gave names, addresses, and telephone numbers for seventeen book-publishing firms.

Other gambits include checking the card catalogue of the nearest university library for books in your research area to see who is publishing what and consulting the annual *Writer's Market.* Historical quarterlies may give you a lead in the review section. Periodicals like the New Mexico Book League's quarterly *Book Talk*[18] and *Books of the Southwest,* issued monthly by University of Arizona Librarian W. David Laird,[19] are full of information about small presses. The June, 1978, issue of *Books of the Southwest* reviewed thirty-four titles. Only ten bore the imprint of major publishers. Nine carried press names obviously thought up by self-publishers or small-press entrepreneurs: Padma Press, Oatman, Arizona; Rainbow Expeditions, Tucson. Six were established small presses (Sunstone Press, Santa Fe; Nortex Press, then of Quanah, Texas, now of Burnet; Cordovan Publications, Houston, book-publishing division of *Horseman* magazine). The rest were in-house reports or bulletins issued by technical, municipal, and other groups.

A year later (February, 1980), of thirty titles reviewed, only four were issued by eastern publishers. Seven were by well-known university or regional presses. The rest were fathered by such organizations as the Flagstaff Corral of the Westerners, the National Park Service, and the Grand Canyon Natural History Association. The conclusion is inescapable that an amazing variety of publishing outlets exists in the Southwest and elsewhere. Self-publishing and small-press publishing are here to stay and offer real opportunities to the regional historian.

The West Coast has attracted a small army of examples, and business has boomed since the early sixties. A pioneer organization was Dustbooks, which started in 1963 as a literary magazine (*Dust*) but soon developed into a multifaceted publication enterprise. It issued three annuals: *The International Directory of Little Magazines and Small Presses, Directory of Small Magazine/Press Editors and Publishers,* and *The Small Press Record of Books in Print.* Dustbooks also published novels, poetry, nonfiction, anthologies, and how-to books and operated a small-press book club. Three of its titles related to self-publishing—for example, *How to Publish Your Own Book,* by L. W. Mueller, originally issued by Arlo Press. A somewhat similar organization was COSMEP (Committee of

Small Editors and Publishers) WEST, which merged in 1978 with Literary Publishers of Southern California to form Western Independent Publishers (WIP). Neither Dustbooks nor Western Independent Publishers made a specialty of historical writing, but both recognized its existence and gave it limited coverage, particularly if the writers showed liberal leanings. *Sipapu*, the WIP newsletter, announced its special interest in "alternative publications, including Third World, dissent, feminist, self-reliant and underground publications." A regional historian with the right interests (blacks, chicanos, women's liberation, the counter culture) could find a home with these or other liberal-radical publishers and distributors, who proliferated in California and neighboring states in the seventies and early eighties.[20]

The expansion was so rapid, in fact, as to deserve the term "explosion," and it was the same in other parts of the country. The American Booksellers Association convention in Chicago in the early summer of 1980 was "an upbeat ABA for small presses," and many of them used it as a "launching pad." Such a battalion of them was present that for the first time "small press" proved to be "too vague and limiting a category for so many commercial, literary, regional and specialized publishing exhibitors."[21]

The trend was particularly strong in the Pacific states and created a need for a directory listing all the houses, big and little, new and old, doing business in the region, and two such directories were available in 1980: *A Writer's Guide to West Coast Publishing*, by Frances Halpern (Hwong Publishing Company, 10353 Los Alamitos Blvd., Los Alamitos, California 90720, $10.95), and a catalogue issued by the Northwest Book Publishers Association (P.O. Box 122, Seattle, Washington 98111).[22]

Better marketing facilities accompanied the small-publishing boom, creating greater opportunities for the regional historian once he achieved publication. Some small western presses went so far as to become distributors themselves, listing books issued by other firms along with their own. Jean Jones of Laramie, Wyoming, started her Jelm Mountain Publications in 1974, specializing in regional poetry, fiction, and nonfiction, but her 1980 list of

157 titles was divided about equally between her own books and those of other presses. An intriguing item (no. 142) was Jane Cannary Hickok's *Calamity Jane's Letters to Her Daughter,* published in 1976 by the Shameless Hussy Press.[23]

An interesting "new phenomenon" on the West Coast was the growth of a distributing system to meet "the intensified competition among regional small-press and specialized wholesalers." *Publishers Weekly* in May, 1980, noted the rapid expansion of Pacific Pipeline of Seattle and Publishers Group West of Emeryville, California. "Within a few years," said Charlie Winton of PWG, "the quality of small press books from the West has improved so incredibly that when you place them alongside books published by major publishers, you can no longer tell the difference."[24]

Encouraging in another way was the announcement in August, 1980, of the appearance of *Free Lance West: A Monthly Newsletter for and About Writers in the West.* Norm Bolotin and Charles W. Gordon, coeditors, assured the regional writer: "We will tell you about a new magazine in Oregon, weekly newspapers in Alaska, fiction contests in Washington, new book publications in British Columbia, and so on. We will tell you about what publishers want and what they're buying; when new publications start up and when they're belly up."[25]

With all these systems go, as the astronauts phrase it, one important button remains to be pushed: the budding regional writer must first make sure he has something to communicate — something that will be interesting to a reasonable number of nonprofessionals. The next step is to make it publishable. A great many amateur (and some professional) historians need help in this department. If the would-be writer has no training in composition and no particular talent for it, he should turn for aid to someone who has both. Editors of journals will sometimes give a manuscript a face-lifting operation; publishers of books ordinarily will not. All but the least socially acceptable historians, however, have friends and acquaintances with the required skills who can be persuaded — or paid — to come to the rescue. Many a fine researcher cannot produce a publishable manuscript without help, and he should not be ashamed to ask for it.

The final move is to start the end product on its travels and keep it going until it finds a home. The great mistake is to let it settle down in a filing cabinet or gather dust on a desk. A man who gives up after the first rejection may be overly modest—"Who am I to compete with James Michener?"—though this is not a common failing. Sometimes he is so afraid of being caught in error that he does not really want to let his manuscript get out of his hands. The late Maurice Garland Fulton, the historian of Lincoln County, New Mexico, and its wars, wrote three versions of his history of the area and left them when he died for Robert Mullin to sort out and combine in *Maurice G. Fulton's History of the Lincoln County War*. He made no serious attempt to look for a publisher himself.

Another nonpublisher is the academician who uses his project as a crutch or security blanket. Everybody knows that he is working on the Rocky Mountain fur trade—has been deeply immersed in it for ten, fifteen, twenty years. He has published an article or two, but the major work is always just over the horizon, and remains so—necessarily. As long as it remains to be completed, his standing as a scholar is secure. "Oh, yes, Sonovitch," his colleagues say. "You know he has a long-range project going on the fur trade. We try not to overload him." So he keeps it going because, if he did not, his career and possibly his life would be over.

It may be necessary for an unpublished historian to reason with himself if modesty or fear of criticism is holding him back (the security-blanket researcher is hopeless), but he must not expect too much. Historical writing seldom approaches romance or pornography in popular appeal, but it does have a market. Let the author beware, however, of setting his sights too high. It is better to be content with the lower rungs of the ladder than to aim high and fall flat.

5

A Book Is Born

A View from the Delivery Room

WRITING A BOOK and getting it published are much like having a baby. Before you have it, parenthood seems like a pinnacle of bliss. After you have it, you count your pains as well as your pleasures. Similarly, a man trying to get his first book printed can conceive of no greater happiness than seeing his thoughts in type. Then it happens, and his eyes are opened.

The parallels start at the moment of conception. Love has prepared the way—a deep affection for what seems like a wonderful subject. Nature takes its course, and the great idea begins to grow in the mental womb of the potential author. Note cards accumulate, features take shape, and signs of pregnancy become visible in the form of preoccupation, impatience with his wife when she recommends diversion, a growing conviction that the world is waiting for his product as it awaits the sunrise.

It is a time of worry and frustration. If you write fiction, your best friend observes that fiction is not selling and you ought to go in for history. If you write history, he suggests that fiction would be better. Time drags; worldly concerns interfere. Book pregnancies have no fixed terminal date, and ten years, twenty years, may go by before the child is ready to be born. Real motherhood is not as difficult.

Then there is the possibility of a miscarriage. When Carlyle's only copy of *The French Revolution* was destroyed in a fire, he gave all subsequent writers something to shudder about. It *can* happen to anybody, and many pregnant authors have had narrow escapes. Elmer Edgar Stoll, who taught Shakespeare at the University of Minnesota when I was an undergraduate there, was working on a manuscript and kept his papers at his office in Folwell Hall. One night he dreamed that the building had caught fire and his book was in danger. He threw on some clothes and walked five miles in the small hours of early morning to make sure that his dream was false. Pregnant people do things like that.

The hardest part is finding an obstetrician — that is, a publisher. This midwife has a staff of assistants who look into the matter and determine whether the proposed birth is worth arranging for. If your tome has any pretensions to scholarship, it will go to an "expert" in your field, and he will have every reason to reject you and cut your heart out in the process. If you have written a good book, a better one than he could have written, he will hate you and tear you to pieces. If you go against his special prejudices and persuasions, he will accuse you of ignorance and willful error. If you agree with him in any important detail, he may accuse you of plagiarizing the idea from him. If he is a nit-picker and he can find a few typos, he will rejoice greatly and write the editor at length pointing out your subhuman qualities.

The worst thing you can do is to get crosswise with an anthropologist. Nobody can be as cantankerous and intransigent as one of these creatures. When I wrote a book about the Mescalero Apaches some years ago, the manuscript went off to a nationally known anthropologist who is famous for his dog-in-the-manger attitudes. The publishers sent his report to me with his name left off, but I knew who did it. He left no adjective unturned and concluded with the opinion that I was unable to use the English language in an acceptable manner. His condemnation was so sweeping and wholehearted that the University of Oklahoma Press rejected his advice and printed the book in spite of him. It is now in its fourth printing.

I once suspected the late Stanley Vestal of the University of Oklahoma of dissecting a manuscript of mine with some ruthlessness, and when I had the good fortune to spend a night at his house in Norman, I took pains to express my opinion of publishers' readers who confuse themselves with God Almighty and hurl thunderbolts at defenseless authors. He convinced me that I was wrong.

"Readers," he said, "are not employed for the purpose of patting authors on the head. Their business is to pick flaws. If they miss something and the reviewers jump on it after publication, the fat is in the fire. So they look for every possible weakness. It is their job, and they do it."

I apologized and backed off. But no mother likes to have these assistant midwives poking and probing to see if she is going to have a healthy, interesting child. They may be necessary, but they can hurt. And each obstetrician that one approaches has a staff of his own, and the job has to be done again. The strange part of it is that the probers and pokers never agree among themselves. They hardly ever think that you are going to have a healthy infant; one says it is too short, another one says it is too long, a third says there are better examples of this sort of infant already in circulation.

While they are arguing, a new worry presents itself. For some reason which has not yet been explored or explained, two or more people get pregnant with the same idea at the same time. It happens all the time, and there is no way two people can have the same baby—not as a rule. Sometimes joint parenthood can be arranged, but usually whoever has been pregnant longer gets to keep the child. There is nothing for the loser to do but try to get pregnant again.

Once your pregnancy has been approved and you have secured the services of an obstetrician, you can go to the hospital at the proper time and begin labor. Here again your child may or may not be pleasing to the operatives and may or may not have to undergo operations to improve its chances of survival or make it more pleasing to the obstetrician.

It does seem that these technicians (editors) live always in the past. Everything must be done the way it always has been done. No departures from custom and tradition are tolerated without prolonged and sometimes bitter argument. One problem I always have with editors is the location of the acknowledgments. My theory is that acknowledgments, like notes, bibliographies, and indexes, are housekeeping matters and should be tucked away at the back of the book. As few barriers as possible should be placed between the reader and the first page of text. Usually, however, acknowledgments are positioned somewhere near the front for reasons which are now lost in the mists along the River of Time. Unless I watch closely and protest immediately and vigorously when the copy editor starts moving my thank-you's from the back to the beginning, I am likely to find myself conforming in spite of my convictions. If I relax my vigilance, I get galley proofs with footnotes at the bottom of the page instead of at the back, and when I protest, my editor says, "You didn't *say* you wanted backnotes." And since we are already in galleys, I am helpless.

These specialists have all sorts of fixed ideas which they will give up only after prolonged controversy. One of them once insisted that "for instance" was wrong and that "for example" was right. He could not tell me why, however. Matters like the comma before "and" in a compound sentence or before "and" at the end of a series are as important as the ten commandments, and the hyphenation of compound adjectives before the noun (sacred in my book) can be as important as female chastity.

It is all over eventually, and the book is born, though it may be so long after labor began that the thrill of parenthood is gone. I know of one author—an anthropologist—whose book was accepted five years ago and might not be out yet if his wife had not gone to the obstetrician and demanded that something be done. "This man," she said, "has cancer and may not be here long. You will have to get this book out or I am going to do something about it." The obstetrician induced labor at once.

When you hold your offspring in your hands, it looks good to you, but you cannot be sure what you have produced. It may be stillborn or an idiot. The reviewers are the ones to tell you about that, and you have to remain calm and impassive, like an Indian at the stake, while they apply the torch. There are fair and intelligent ones, like W. H. Hutchinson of California and Alice Bullock of New Mexico, but you run the risk of getting the other kind. If your reviewer has never written a book himself, you can be in deep trouble. Old bachelors always know more about babies than mothers do. A reviewer who has produced something himself and knows about the perils and pitfalls and frustrations is apt to be more tolerant and understanding than a nonproducer. The worst fate, however, is to draw a reviewer who is tremendously successful and is in great demand as a writer, lecturer, and reviewer. He never has time to read your book and sometimes has no real idea of what it is all about. I could name some important figures who have reviewed books of mine — unfavorably — without getting past page ten. One famous fellow, now dead, concluded his review of *Cowboys and Cattle Kings: Life on the Range Today* (1950) with the remark, "This is not the book to end all books about the cowboy." Since the thing had no objective beyond describing the state of the cattlemen in 1949, I suspected that the great man had not tried to find out what the volume was all about.

And while the reviewers are working your infant over, the letters begin to come in pointing out your errors. Some show a childish joy in catching you off base. Some are written in a spirit of kindness and helpfulness. In either case one has to be grateful for them, for no matter how much care and feeding go into the production, some things are going to be wrong. It is the human condition. Marshall Townsend, director of the University of Arizona Press, says that with all the reading and rereading that go into the production of one of his books, an average of seven typos per volume is the rule. Perfectionists find it difficult to adjust to this fact of life. I once wrote a history of the State National Bank of El Paso in collaboration with Millard McKinney, who learned to be a perfectionist in the course of years of service with the United States Navy in charge of aircraft maintenance. He was unusually gifted as a picture specialist, turning out good work and labeling everything with meticulous correctness. When the book was in my hands, I opened it to a photograph of a circus parade headed west on Mills Street past Pioneer Plaza. The caption said, "Circus parade coming east on St. Louis Street (now Mills) and turning into Little Plaza (now Pioneer Plaza) circa 1885." I called McKinney and told him what I was looking at. He checked for himself and said, as he hung up the telephone, "I want to die."

In one respect an author is fortunate to locate these inevitable errors. When a soldier makes a mistake, he may get shot. When a football player makes a mistake, he may lose the game. When a golfer makes a mistake, it may cost him $50,000. An author, however, sometimes has a chance to play his shot over — to correct his error — to be, if we keep the metaphor, born again. If there is a second printing, it is a new ball game, a new life.

This chance of going through the delivery room a second time is perhaps the best thing about a business which is frustrating, discouraging, defeating, and sometimes maddening. If and when we get to heaven, we will probably find a few authors there, but the successful and popular ones will be missing. If they have gone into multiple printings, Saint Peter will say when they present themselves at the gate, "Go away! You have had your heaven. We need the room for the fellow who didn't get past the first printing."

6

Victims of Time

The American Pioneers
and the Western Historian

WE RODE INTO TOWN with care," says the viewpoint character of Louis L'Amour's western novel *The Lonely Men*, "for we were all men with enemies:"

> The temperature was over a hundred in the shade.
> "All this town needs," John J. Battles said, "is more water and a better class of people."
> "That's all hell needs," Spanish replied.[1]

The town Tell Sackett and his friends invaded in 1870 or thereabouts was Tucson, Arizona. Tell adds: "Although we spoke so lightly of Tucson, we all liked the town and were glad to be there."

Other early-day observers seem to have agreed almost 100 percent with John J. Battles's sentiments about the Old Pueblo and its pioneer citizens, and few of them were "glad to be there." Mina Oury, who arrived in November, 1865, called the adobe village "the most forlorn, dreary, desolate, God-forsaken spot of earth ever trodden by the foot of a white man," and J. Ross Browne, who came in the middle sixties, declared that "if the world were searched over, there could not be found so degraded a set of villains as formed the principal society of Tucson."[2]

It would seem impossible to go beyond these sweeping condemnations, but even worse things are being said in our time about our pioneer ancestors, not just in Arizona but in all parts of the West. If those old-timers could come back and listen to their detractors, they would not believe their own ears. Had they

48

been indifferent to the opinions of posterity, their fall from grace would be more understandable, but they really wanted the approval of future generations and felt that they had earned it. In 1884 they founded the Arizona Pioneers Historical Society to preserve in memory the trials and triumphs of the firstcomers— Anglos, of course. Indian and Mexican pioneers were not included.

In every western state, and I know of no exceptions, similar groups of early settlers organized just before or just after the turn of the century and set up libraries, museums, and biographical files to make sure they would not be forgotten by posterity. In one sense they were successful, for posterity has not forgotten them. The honor and respect which they coveted, however, has been denied them, and in our days their credit is at the lowest ebb ever. The business of the western historian is to record their triumphs and defeats, and until recently he could do it with sympathy and approval. Times have changed, however, and now the early settlers are in such disrepute that a chronicler who gives them any credit at all is in danger of being branded with guilt by association.

State historical societies are key organizations in this anomalous situation, and the pioneers who founded them are focal points of praise and blame. The Arizona Pioneers Historical Society, now the Arizona Historical Society (the pioneers were left out in 1971), is probably more or less typical. It was the child of an assembly calling itself the Society of Arizona Pioneers which gathered at the Palace Hotel in Tucson on January 31, 1884. The possibility of forming such an organization had been discussed for some time, and preliminary meetings had been held in the home of Jacob Mansfeld. The call for the first assembly was issued by Charles D. Poston, a sharp and salty fellow who spent his life trying to get rich in Arizona and never made it. Over 100 sent regrets, and 145 showed up.[3]

The first session was peaceful, but the second, held on February 9, 1885, was explosive. Violent differences of opinion arose about who should be admitted as members. The suggestion was made that only those who arrived before January 1, 1870, should be eligible. Poston wanted to admit anybody who came before 1876, the centennial year. Jacob Mansfeld proposed that the cut-off date be April 30, 1871 – the date of the Camp Grant Massacre, "when the people of Arizona protected themselves from the Indians."[4] This successful attempt to exterminate a whole camp of Apaches consisting mostly of old men, women, and children seemed to Jacob an occasion for celebration thirteen years after the event. Others preferred March 20, 1880, the day the railroad reached Tucson. The date finally agreed on was January 1, 1870.

That left many of those present outside the fold, and a hundred of them walked out. Charles Poston, highly incensed, withdrew also and asked that his name be removed from the list of members. His request was honored, but his fellow pioneers refused to give him up entirely. They made him an honorary member, and his name appears as founder of the club on a bronze plaque at the Tucson headquarters.

The members agreed that the society was intended to serve "historical and humanitarian purposes" and to "perpetuate the memory of those whose sagacity, energy and enterprise induced them to settle in the wilderness and become the founders of a new state."[5]

The association was in many ways a true fraternity. Past perils and hardships brought the members close to each other (when they were not engaged in furious debate), and they sometimes called each other brother. When one of them died, the others felt his passing as a personal loss, turned out for the funeral, and comforted the survivors. They set up a Widow and Orphan Fund for the relief of those survivors, an Indian Depredation Fund, and a library where the life stories of the true pioneers could be preserved along with books and manuscripts related to early times. Like other brotherhoods, they believed that one member's misdoings reflected on all, and they insisted that every man's record should be above reproach. "Members guilty of misconduct," said one of the bylaws, "may be expelled from the Society." Minor offenses might be punished by fine or reprimand. Nothing in the records indicates that anyone was ever ejected from membership, or even reproved, but it is clear that the founders were serious in calling their brotherhood a "Moral, Benevolent, Literary and Scientific Association," with emphasis on "Moral."[6]

They even demanded good manners. Decent conduct in meetings was enjoined, probably to prevent a recurrence of the uproar at the second meeting: "In debate no member shall be personal in his remarks."[7]

Since a fraternity by definition must fraternize, and since theirs was intended, as their charter states, "to cultivate social intercourse and form a more perfect union" among members, they sponsored an active social program — monthly meetings climaxed by an annual banquet and ball.

Here and there throughout the West in due time similar groups came together with similar objectives. These were not the pioneer assemblies we hear about — miners' meetings, lynching parties, kangaroo courts. The members were proud and decent people, asking for a place in history. In 1884, obviously, the Arizona pioneers were confident of the value of their achievements. They considered themselves as forerunners of civilization who had endured and sacrificed much in the public interest. They felt that they were entitled to the thanks of posterity and had no doubt that posterity would want to know of their experiences.

Their sense of mission was strong, as one would expect. Addressing the membership on his retirement from the presidency on December 29, 1885, H. S. Stevens delivered "a few appropriate remarks" which were made part of the society's records:

My Fellow Pioneers: . . . my remarks must be few, but believe me, they express the cherished sentiments of a pioneer's heart, one, my Brother Pioneers, who like you rejoices in the knowledge that the members of our Society were the first to bring American civilization to the savages of this country, and with those who arrived since the Pioneer days, have freely and fearlessly sustained it by their means and their best efforts.

   To our children who are to take our places in the coming time . . .we hopefully transmit this knowledge and all other blessings that may result from the "Pioneer days" in the "sun-kissed land" of Arizona.[8]

Reading this paragraph almost a century later, one has to wonder whether Hiram Stevens could possibly have been serious. The Camp Grant Massacre, which seems to us now such a terrible blot on the record of the early settlers, had occurred only a few years before. William S. Oury, first president of the society, had joined the party of "ninety-two Papagos, forty-eight Mexicans and six Americans" who had wiped out the Apache camp. So far as I can determine, only three men who became members of the society went along, but there can be no doubt that the Anglo population of Tucson approved of what Oury and Jesús María Elías did on the morning of April 29, 1871. Hiram Stevens stayed in Tucson, but he responded to a request from Oury and dispatched a party to the Cañada del Oro on the main road to Camp Grant to make sure a messenger from Camp Lowell did not get through with a warning.[9] How could Stevens, with this record behind him, talk about "bringing American civilization to the savages of this country"?

The words made perfectly good sense to him and his friends. In their minds the massacre was a punitive measure intended to stop the Apaches from committing any more depredations. The outlying districts were in an uproar. Whites were being slaughtered right and left by raiding bands. Something had to be done, and they did it. It was not, they thought, as though the Indians had no chance of bettering themselves. The blessings of American civilization were available to them any time they wished to give up their wild life, stay on the reservations provided for them, and behave the way the Americans wanted them to. Nobody in 1885 had the smallest suspicion that the Apache lifeway was a beautiful thing, superior to that of the white man. Not one could possibly foresee that a century later his descendants would put all the blame on him, making him responsible for all the suffering and bloodshed.

That, however, is what has happened. The roles have been reversed. The pioneers are now the bad guys. The Indians are on the side of the angels. They attuned their lives to the rhythms of nature, lived in harmony with their environment, respected the earth they lived on. A great many people who are sick of white civilization, or think they are, take all this seriously and modify their own life-style accordingly. They go barefoot, eat granola, and let the wind blow through their beards. They do not, however, abandon their bathrooms and refrigerators.

The movement has been growing for at least a century. The Doolittle Commission of 1865 sent observers to the reservations and reported to Congress that the Indians had been betrayed and abused by the white man.[10] In fiction, which is always a good barometer, sympathetic pictures of Indian life appeared in 1889 in Adolph F. A. Bandelier's *The Delight Makers* and in 1907 in Marah Ellis Ryan's *Indian Love Letters*.[11] The noble Apache arrived as early as 1923 in Harold Bell Wright's *The Mine with the Iron Door*, set in the Santa Catalina Mountains near Tucson.[12] The educated Apache Natachee gave the white man full credit for the woes of his people. Edgar Rice (Tarzan) Burroughs beat the drum even louder in 1927 in *Apache Devil*, which makes Geronimo out to be a fine humanitarian philosopher and portrays most of the white men as trash.[13] The big push came, however, with Elliott Arnold's *Blood Brother* in 1947.[14] The viewpoint character is Tom Jeffords, who in the flesh was a charter member of the Arizona Pioneers Historical Society, but the real hero is Cochise, the great Apache chief. He is portrayed as a statesman and poet—a noble human being much superior to the white men who make trouble for him.

The trend continued, and by 1961, when Jane Barry wrote her well-received novel *A Time in the Sun*, the whole picture had been turned upside down.[15] The Apaches were now the people to admire, kindly souls goaded past bearing by the wicked whites, and the wicked whites were the ones who did the deeds Indians were supposed to do—raping, murdering, and scalping.

In the 1960s the country followed the trail marked out by Arnold and Barry. The cause became, in fact, a bandwagon, and everybody tried to get on it. The nineteenth-century Apaches were not savages any more. They were preindustrials. Their culture and religion were superior to anything the whites had produced, and this idea became an article of faith among intelligent, liberal-minded people throughout the country. The public was ready when Dee Brown in *Bury My Heart at Wounded Knee* quoted "words of gentle reasonableness coming from the mouths of Indians stereotyped in American myth as ruthless savages" and set out to show that "the intruders from the East were determined to destroy all that was Indian as well as America itself."[16] Readers listened when Black Elk of the Oglala Sioux spoke:

> Once we were happy in our own country and we were seldom hungry, for then the two-leggeds and the four-leggeds lived together like relatives, and there was plenty for them and for us. But the Wasichus came, and they have made little islands for us and other little islands for the four-leggeds, and always these islands are becoming smaller, for around them surges the gnawing flood of the Wasichu; and it is dirty with lies and greed.[17]

The pioneers started it. They opened the door, took the land, broke the treaties, penned the tribesmen on reservations. Chief Luther Standing Bear of the Sioux sums it up:

> We did not think of the great open plains, the beautiful rolling hills, and winding streams with tangled growth as "wild". . . . Not until the hairy man from the east came and with brutal frenzy heaped injustices upon us and the families we loved was it "wild" for us. When the very animals of the forest began fleeing from his approach, then it was that for us the "Wild West" began.[18]

Two centuries after the Republic was founded, most of us appear to believe that we stole the country from its real possessors. We accept as truth books like Wilbur Jacobs's *Dispossessing the American Indian* (1972) and Wendell H. Oswaldt's *This Land Was Theirs* (1966, 1973), and we spend many millions of dollars trying to atone for what we have done.[19] To me this seems like trying to buy our way out of a bad situation, and I suspect that all this money heaped upon peoples unprepared to handle it has done as much harm as good, but posterity will have to be the judge of that.

Meanwhile we seem to feel that we have two alternatives: pay up or give the country back to the Indians. Some militant Indian groups, like some militant chicano groups (who also think a considerable part of the country belongs to them), would like to reclaim selected portions of the territory. Nasnaga's 1975 novel, *Indians' Summer*, shows how it might be done. We cannot, however, even consider giving up the United States.[20] There would be no place for three hundred million ugly Americans to go. Nobody would have us. We would have to dispossess somebody else in order to live. Besides, it is doubtful that the Indians would know what to do with Phoenix or Los Angeles.

Probably this idea is not being taken seriously because there is another way. We can join the Indians. In fact, a great chorus of advisers tells us that the white man is doomed because he has lost touch with his environment—that his only hope is to return to the Indian's way of living and thinking. Mabel Dodge Luhan declared in *Edge of Taos Desert* (1937) that the future of the white man lay with "the Indian Americas," but she was a rich, dissatisfied white woman who had gone to live with the Taos tribe, and nobody took her seriously.[21] Thirty-five years later, however, Vine Deloria said the same thing in *God Is Red*, and everybody seemed inclined to agree.[22] We were already convinced in 1976, when Stan Steiner (*The Vanishing White Man*) quoted an Iroquois woman named Doris Melliadis:

> Now they come to gather for the coming disaster and destruction of the white man *by his own hands*, with his progressive, advanced, technological devices, that only the American Indian can avert. Now the time is near. And it is only the Indian who knows the cure. It is only the Indian who can stop this plague.[23]

This is the point at which we have arrived ninety years after Hiram Stevens spoke with such pride of the achievement of his generation in bringing "American civilization to the savages of this country." Has any other nation in the history of the world behaved in this fashion, beating its breast, denying its right to exist, reviling its ancestors, acknowledging its inferiority? Probably not.

What has happened to cause this phenomenon? At the root of it, in all probability, is an enormous and universal dissatisfaction with the United States of America and what it is supposed to stand for. Crime, corruption, and violence in the streets alarm us. The ecologists and conservationists have their own legitimate sources of dissatisfaction with our treatment of the land and our national resources. The blacks, the chicanos, and the militant Indians accuse the white majority of high crimes against the minority groups. To make matters worse, we have been so prosperous as a nation that we feel guilty about it. When we are in danger or under stress, we struggle and strive and have faith and give our all cheerfully, but when we are at peace and enjoy the best of everything, we suffer. Nobody—and this is a basic truth—can be as discouraged and depressed as a man who has it made. Naturally, since we are doing pretty well, at least for the moment, we have given up hope for the country.

A story has been going around about a man who was driving across the Bay Bridge to San Francisco one morning and was horrified to see a fellow human being climbing on the railing with the obvious intention of jumping off. He stopped his car, got out, and climbed up alongside the potential suicide. "What in the world has gone wrong with you?" he asked. "What could make you want to do a thing like this?"

"The world is in a terrible mess. I can't stand it any longer. I just don't want to go on living in such a madhouse."

"Well, wait just a minute. Give me five minutes to tell you what is right with the world. Then I'll give you five minutes to tell me what is wrong."

The man agreed. They each took five minutes. Then they both jumped.

Given these ingredients—enthusiasm for the Indian way of life, rejection of our own, guilt feelings about the westward movement, desire to atone for it—and nothing good can be said about Hiram Stevens, William S. Oury, and their generation of pioneers. The Arizona Historical Society in its printed history still says that its aim is to create "a greater awareness of and appreciation of the hardships and self-sacrifices of those who conquered the wilderness and established civilization," but such language is not often heard in the second half of the twentieth century. What we get now is passages like this one from John Upton Terrell's *Apache Chronicle* (1972):

> Paeans of praise continue to ring loudly for the brave souls who set off into the unknown deserts with a burning dream of helping to build a greater America.
> They didn't do any such thing. They thought least of all about the future of their country, and this was true of Spaniards and Mexicans as much as it was of Americans. The only dreams any of them had, aside from nightmares caused by fear, were of gold, silver, and free land, of getting rich with a minimum of exertion and little or no expense to themselves.

The final defeat of the desert Indians, Terrell says, "was accomplished by the perfidy, the treachery, the inhumanity of bestial white civilians, both in Washington and the Southwest, forces which created in them a hopelessness which they were unable to combat." The pioneers, by and large, were "uncouth, ignorant, bigoted, and looking for something for nothing."[24] This is strong language, but Terrell is, of course, partly right. The frontier was not peopled by aristocrats, professional men, highly educated people, or fine gentlemen, though these did appear. Even so, the early settlers were not necessarily "the dregs of their respective societies," as Terrell says. Frontier towns were often short on law and order, it is true, but when the "dregs of their respective societies" were run out or buried, they ceased to be frontier towns.

What Terrell, Dee Brown, Vine Deloria and the rest forget or overlook is the presence in every pioneer community, even in Tucson, where a "degraded set of villains" formed "the principal society," of a hard core of good, conscientious, public-spirited people. And some of them had excellent backgrounds. They did not and could not think the way we do, but the best of them were far above average.

Take Peter R. Brady, Arizona pioneer. He was born in 1825 in

Georgetown, District of Columbia. His father was a close friend of Andrew Jackson and served as presidential secretary. Peter himself started his career as a midshipman in the United States Navy. He was at home in Washington, but he was just as much at home in Texas, Mexico, California, and Arizona, where he served his country well. He and others like him were frontiersmen because they liked the new country and its challenges — not because they were out of place in civilized society.[25]

William S. Oury came of a long-established eastern family, longtime residents of western Virginia.[26] Others of the sixty-two charter members of the Arizona Pioneers Historical Society came from substantial stock and were well educated for their time and place.

Such people were responsible and conscientious, and their opinions about themselves and their conduct should not be taken lightly. If Hiram Stevens did not see anything incongruous in his "appropriate remarks," already quoted, there had to be a reason. If Bill Oury could read a paper on the Camp Grant Massacre to the membership of the Arizona Pioneers Historical Society, as he did on April 6, 1885, without embarrassment, there had to be a reason.[27] It is true that Sidney R. DeLong, trader and businessman who participated in the Camp Grant affair, said in his old age that the one thing he regretted in his life was this slaughter, in which the innocent suffered with the guilty, but nobody, while the Apache menace was a present reality, regretted what had happened.[28] It seemed to those involved that it was something that had to be done. They were wrong, we firmly believe, but they did not know it at the time. When some of their descendants dropped a bomb on Hiroshima, they did not know it either.

When we condemn the pioneers, we are assuming that their motives and their information were the same as ours. No historian worthy of the name should fall into this trap. He should be able to examine the policies of his predecessors dispassionately without approving of their actions. In every corner of the West such examination is necessary if the search for truth is to continue — if our forebears are to face the spotlight of history with any credit at all.

It should be obvious that both sides, Indians and pioneers alike, had the same motives — the defense of their homes and the support of their families. We give the Apaches credit for skill and determination in carrying out their objectives, though we do not go along with some of their methods. The pioneers should get credit for the skill and determination with which they carried out *their* objectives, though we cannot go along with some of their methods either. There were good people and bad people on both sides.

It is hard to say what the percentage of good citizens was on the frontier, even if one could arrive at a satisfactory definition of a "good citizen." I once asked Farrington Carpenter, an influential Colorado cattleman, what percentage of ranchmen, in his opinion, were honest. He replied, "They are about 2 percent SOBs, just like other people."[29] The percentage of SOBs on the fringes of civilization may have been slightly higher than 2 percent, but there are no statistics. At least not everybody was a thief and a murderer.

Perhaps the question might not seem so puzzling and complicated if one could realize that much more is involved here than simple matters of right and wrong, truth and falsehood. To make intelligent judgments, one has to go back a long way and observe the human race in operation. One has to watch the Jews overrunning the Land of Canaan, justified by their own brand of manifest destiny; the Romans expanding their empire and rolling the Picts and the Scots back beyond Hadrian's Wall; the Pilgrims landing at Plymouth and dispossessing the Indians in the name of God; the Indians themselves overrunning each other — the Athapascans filtering down from the north and evicting the Hohokam or the Anasazi or whoever was there ahead of them. The whole history of mankind has been a succession of folk movements — invasions and dispossessions. People moved, and still move, like water seeking a level, and not always by conquest. The flood of "illegal aliens" coming up from Mexico as this is written is not militant, but it is as real — and probably as justifiable — as the winning of the West.

Walter Prescott Webb called the westward movement of the

European peoples over the last four hundred years an irresistible drive toward new country—the Great Frontier—where there was food, freedom, and land.[30] One could talk about right and wrong in connection with such movements if the men involved had power of choice. The individual pioneer, however, could not see beyond the assumptions of his time and his group or resist the tides which bore him on. His "world-view," in a favorite phrase of our generation, was part of his original equipment; his feelings about what he was doing were the feelings of his generation.

I once heard a thoughtful man with an interest in history speak of the "frenzy" which takes hold of ordinary people when their world is on the move—in 1849, for example, when half the United States, it seemed, was on the road to California.[31] The frenzy was real, and it was highly contagious.

There was never any difficulty about rationalizing what was done. The Romans brought the Pax Romana to the peoples they conquered and claimed credit for civilizing them. The British brought the Pax Britannica without using the term. It was not really necessary to have an excuse. The Northmen had no qualms about moving into England when the Romans withdrew and left it unprotected. The Comanches, so far as we know, did not search their souls before chasing the Eastern Apaches into Mexico at the beginning of the eighteenth century. Not until the twentieth century did whole nations discover that they had taken what did not belong to them and decided to give it back, or at least pay for it. This eccentric conduct has already cost the United States many millions of dollars. In Africa it opened the door for Idi Amin.

The individual pioneer, of course, seldom if ever thought of himself as part of a folk movement. He was too busy surviving to do much meditating about his role in history. Mostly he was an ordinary fellow with extraordinary problems, and he should not be either idealized or lumped with the "dregs of society." He should be looked at with tolerance and some amusement. I once visited a cattleman at the end of a dirt road in the back country of Colorado where conditions were about as primitive as they were in Arizona in 1870, though there was no danger from Indians. When I asked him how he was making out, he replied, "We're doing all right. What we've got here is a lot of brush and some good neighbors, but we get by." There spoke the frontier American.

One summer in Alaska I heard the pioneer in that country described as "a man with a hammer and a saw and a sense of humor." Of the settlers in the Globe area of central Arizona another man said, "They were just ordinary people trying to get along."

In such odd phrases one comes close to the real spirit of the western pioneers. One aspect, however, needs final emphasis: their sense of their role in American history and their hope that they would not be victims of Time and Progress. William S. Oury put the hope into words on March 28, 1880, when he spoke to an assembly gathered to welcome the railroad to Tucson:

> Our mission is ended today; here then arises the question, what are you to do with us? The enterprise of such men as now surround me has penetrated every corner of our broad land, and we now have no frontier to which the pioneer may flee to avoid the tramp of civilized progress; moreover, the weight of years has fallen upon us. Consequently the few remaining years which the Divine Master may have in store for us must be spent amongst you; and in the whirl of excitement incident to the race after the precious treasure embedded in our mountain ranges, our last request is that you kindly avoid trampling in the dust the few remaining monuments of the first American settlement of Arizona.[32]

Bill Oury's worst fears have been realized. The reputations of his generation and their "few remaining monuments" have been and are being "trampled into dust." The society which he helped to found still functions, however, and so do similar societies in every western state. They are doing all they can to preserve the physical survivals of pioneer times and collect the written records. The real need, nevertheless, is a salvage operation on the pioneers themselves—victims of time and change and the guilt complexes of their descendants.

7

John Doe, OHM

LIKE MOST OTHER AMERICANS, historians have displayed a passion for organization. There is a historical society for everybody, and many of us belong to half a dozen—local, state, regional, and national. There are historical fraternities whose members enter the sacred portals only on invitation. There are supersocieties, like the Society for State and Local History which keeps watch and ward over the historical hinterlands, the boondocks and borderlands of the national experience. There are groups with genealogical, economic, military, and literary emphases. Any history buff who cannot find soul food and fellowship among these clans is an intellectual Robinson Crusoe, and anybody who proposes that another group is needed would seem to be a real eccentric. I rise to suggest, however, that we need another one. It could be called the Order of Minor Historians (OHM) with a bow to the Franciscans (OFM: Order of Friars Minor).

The societies we have now are mostly run by professionals, persons with degrees and training and records of significant publication. They can stand on their own feet, and have been known to stand on the feet of others in their fields of special interest, but the rest of us are amateurs whose presence at conventions is desirable but not vital. Our warm bodies and our financial support are welcome, but we have no special standing. We seldom sit on the front row at annual reunions. We are grateful for a kind word and a smile from Professor Row and Dr. Snow. Most of us are devoted researchers on small projects, unable to spend much time in libraries and archival collections. We hope eventually to get out a book or a couple of articles, but do not publish regularly, and when we do get into print, we are content with a small publisher or even (oh, the shame of it!) with a vanity press. We are modest and sincere and earnest and hardworking. We need an organization of our own for the purpose of promoting fellowship, furthering research, and avoiding what is spoken of in our time as an identity crisis.

Since you may not know that you are in danger of any such catastrophe, I should explain that many novelists and dramatists and social thinkers like to portray the average human being as searching and struggling and agonizing over this problem of identity. When the mourners gather about the grave of Willy Lohman in *Death of a Salesman,* one of them sums it all up: "He never knew who he was."[1] The idea is that none of us really knows who he is and each spends his life trying to find out. It seems that in some, perhaps most, cases it might be better not to know who one is. The shock of discovery could be severe. But I am old-fashioned and have learned not to argue with people who have deep convictions about these things. I wish only to make the point that if all of us, including the Minor Historians, are groping for an identity, we had better face the fact at once that we are what we are and act accordingly. A little *esprit de corps* might help us all.

I include myself among the Minor Historians, although I have done a good bit of publication, first because I have come in through the back door (I am an English teacher by profession) and because I am being constantly reminded that my place is below the salt. Every time I finish a book on a western subject and approach a New York publisher hat in hand, he shakes his head and lets me know that he is not sure the thing will sell in Connecticut. If he accepts it, he seems to be doing it in spite of his better judgment. A steady diet of this sort of treatment does not build confidence, and anyone who has experienced it is likely to be gun-shy—humble and unassuming and grateful for small favors. I ask no more than a membership in the Order of Minor Historians—if they will have me.

The organization, in my judgment, already exists. I have been convinced for a long time that we have an operating fraternity among historical amateurs. Most of us are only dimly aware of it. We have no grips or passwords or initiation ceremonies, but we do have identifying signs and symbols which we recognize and respect. We have a system of professional ethics and a code of conduct which has never been written down, but which determines our attitudes and influences our behavior. We recognize our brothers and sisters in the fraternity. Some special faculty, perhaps connected with the sense of smell, identifies them for us, and we know who does *not* belong by the same process. The fact is, we have developed a half-dozen characteristics which set us apart from any group and give us this feeling of belonging.

The first is a quite extraordinary spirit of helpfulness. We are like the pioneers in the early days of the West, who had to assist each other or perish. When a man was traveling through the country, he expected to stop at any dwelling where night overtook him, and the people in the dwelling expected him to do so. There was no place else to stop, for one thing, and for another those hospitable people might be on the road next week and they would have a right to be entertained too. So it all evened up.

Likewise the Minor Historians could never do their books and monographs on their own. Without help they would take forever to finish their jobs, and they know it. They have a debt to pay, and they gladly pay it. So they form a vast, unorganized Mutual Assistance Society. A man who does not understand this system of give and take is not a member of the Minor Historians, Unincorporated.

I first realized this several years ago when two men from Oklahoma came to see me. One was a well-known western historian, and the other was an oil millionaire who liked being involved with history and bookmaking and got his kicks out of financing and assisting the scholar. These men needed material on the Tularosa country of southern New Mexico, material which I had been accumulating for many years. Some of it I had used in making a book of my own, but there was plenty left, and I handed it over without hesitation, just as some of it had been handed to me. It was, of course, priceless. You cannot evaluate or pay for material like that, and I assumed that my callers knew it.

A few weeks later my millionaire sent me a book, a publication of the University of Oklahoma Press. I didn't need it, but I thought it was nice of him to send it along, and I meant to say thank you when I got time. He could not wait, however. He sent me another copy and a letter complaining that he had received no acknowledgment. Would I please let him know if the first copy had gone astray. He wanted to use the gift as an income-tax deduction.

The letter made me very indignant, and when I analyzed my reaction, I realized that what I resented was the suggestion that he was paying me off. I was about to write him a curt and sarcastic note when I realized that he was not a member of the fraternity and did not know the rules we play by. He was more to be pitied than censured. So I sent back the second copy, thanked him, and let it go at that. He has now gone to his reward, whatever that is for an oilman. I would never say that he has been turned down for membership in the Celestial Petroleum Club, but I am sure he is not in the corner of heaven reserved for the Minor Historians.

This man made me realize the existence of the Minor Historian's Golden Rule: "Do as Much as You Can for Others, Because They Have Already Done Much for You." You can think of plenty of examples of your own of people who have surprised you by not behaving as a Minor Historian should. On the other hand, any one of us could whip up a long list of men and women who have welcomed the stranger and made him feel at home, people who have shared their wealth gladly, ungrudgingly, enthusiastically. I myself have the deepest possible feelings of gratitude to hundreds of them, all over the country—and I am well aware that these debts can never be repaid.

Oftentimes I have felt this way about some act of sharing because generosity was accompanied by considerable sacrifice. I remember that after I had been working for some time on *Roy Bean: Law West of the Pecos*, I decided that I had better make a trip out to Langtry and see what the place looked like. The next evening I found myself part of a pleasant group in the living room of Guy Skiles's home, not far from Roy's old Jersey Lily Saloon. One of the bright spirits present was Dudley Dobie, a former history professor who had become an Americana dealer at San Marcos, Texas. I did not know till many years later that Dudley was visiting in Langtry for the same purpose I was. He too was thinking about writing a book to end all books on Bean. But when he saw that I already had a full head of steam and he was just beginning to stoke his furnace, he left the enterprise to me and gave me all the help he could. Only a member of the fraternity would do this, and I have been proud ever since to recognize Dudley as a fully initiated member of the craft.

Nonmembers do not make these magnificent gestures. In fact, they are likely to be dogs in the manger. When one of us finishes a project and publishes his findings, he often learns that from one to half a dozen specialists have been working on this very book and would have done it better, given a little more time. After I published a work on the Mescalero Apaches, I learned that three other men, longtime residents of the area, had been accumulating material for years and were thinking about beginning to get ready to start a preliminary draft of a book.[2] They resented my snatching their ball and running with it. One of them I considered my friend until he wrote to me commenting on the insufficiencies of my opus, stating that it was not worth much "unless for a satire." I felt unhappy about it but knew that such reactions must be expected from nonmembers of our fraternity.

A second identifying characteristic of the Minor Historian proceeds naturally from the first. As a result of our compulsion to be helpful, we tend to become teachers. Our schools are private ones in which there is no tuition, but the teacher-pupil relationship is almost ideal. I once had such a relationship going with a young Californian who was working on a book about Charleston, Arizona, the ghost town which in the eighties made nearby Tombstone look like a Sunday school. Before Colonel W. C. Greene became a copper king, he lived a few miles up the San Pedro River. The colonel was one of my projects, and when I heard about Jerry, I wrote to him. He shared what he had with me, including a map which I found most useful and transcripts from the local newspapers. It turned out that I could be helpful to him since I had had more experience with such things as footnotes and bibliographies than he had. I gave his manuscript my best efforts and tried to make contact with a publisher for him. Was I being generous? Of course not. I was just keeping the eternal round robin going.

I find that most of us with even limited experience in publication are in this sort of situation all the time. I could tell fifty stories about Minor Historians who have helped me, and I have helped them. My most interesting experiences of this kind, perhaps, have been with members of the English Westerners Society, London Corral. They are all sharp western historians, though few of them have been in the United States. They have familiarized themselves with the basic source material in their special areas of interest, know what is in the state archives, and have microfilms of local and regional newspapers. Depending on voluminous correspondence, they do amazing things.[3]

As the Minor Historian becomes more deeply involved, he finds it impossible to answer all the requests for help. One special problem is the man or woman who comes in with the great news that there is a big story in this old man or that family or such-and-such an old ranch and that the historian is just the one to make a book out of it. The procedure here is obvious. When it happens to me, I tell my visitor to get a tape recorder and a notebook and start collecting. It is his book. The same answer goes for the old-timer who wants me to sit down and record his story — proceeds to be split fifty-fifty. I tell him to write it down or get it on tape and then I will take a hand. Very seldom will one of these people do any work, but when the exception comes along, I help all I can — and sometimes the exception can help me.

Sometimes a man who asks for aid really wants to do something but is not ambitious enough. He hopes to do a little reading in the library and sell a piece to one of the "True" magazines. The treatment for him is to remind him of the work that has already been done and ask what new material he has turned up. If he is a candidate for membership in the organization of Minor Historians, he squirms and fidgets and sometimes goes away mad, but after a few days he comes back and asks, "How do I begin?"

This brings up the third identifying characteristic of the initiate. Once in the fold, he quickly makes his adjustment, like a forest creature taking on the color of its surroundings. He develops a passion for documentation, for one thing, and gets footnote fever in chronic form. He becomes meticulous about sources and references. An unsupported statement is to him the ultimate obscenity, and he will spend days and weeks running down a single note. He is scornful of all journalists, popularizers, clip-and-paste artists, shallow researchers in general. He wants to work at his hobby all the time, and his wife wonders how she can get him to pay a visit or take her out to dinner. His idea of a pleasure trip is a weekend spent in investigating some moldy old ruin or visiting a museum or looking up material in a library somewhere. Of all the oppressed women who could profit by Women's Lib, the wife of the Minor Historian is first and foremost.

It is this dedication, this search for completeness and perfection, that leads to the fourth identifying characteristic of the free and accepted fraternity member. He is always a frustrated man. He is always mistaken about something. He always gets something wrong. There are always typos in his manuscript and errors in his statements of fact. The worst moments come after his book has been published and he is ready to enjoy the fruit of his labors. Then there will be letters in the mail beginning, "Dear Sir: Didn't you know. . . ?" I remember that after *Roy Bean* was off the press I received such a letter. I had said that the west Texas community of Vinegarroon, where Roy had a saloon for a while, was named for "a repulsive but non-poisonous insect" found all over the arid country. "Didn't you know," asked my correspondent, "that a vinegarroon is not an insect but an arachnid, related to the spiders?"[4]

Well, no, I hadn't known that important fact, but now I had learned—the hard way—and I would never be wrong about the vinegarroon again. But I would be wrong about something else. I was wrong when I wrote about the El Paso Salt War, which was fought over the deposits at the base of Guadalupe Peak a hundred miles east of the town. As I got ready to describe the highest mountain in Texas, I thought I could stand a little purple in my prose, so I told how the mountain "lifted its sheer granite wall nine thousand feet above the level plain and the low foothills."[5]

"Didn't you know," the letter said, "that Guadalupe Peak is not igneous in origin but is the largest limestone reef in the world?"

When a woman asked Samuel Johnson why in his dictionary he defined "pastern" as "the knee of a horse," he answered, "Ignorance, Madam, pure ignorance!"[6] About all we can do when we make these mistakes is to follow his example and hope for a second printing. When my book on El Paso history, *Pass of the North*, was issued by TWC Press in 1968, I got so many reminders and found so many errors myself that I sent in two-and-a-half single-spaced pages of corrections for the second edition. And when the revision was out, the first page I turned to had a name misspelled.

Even the most meticulous proofreader misses a few. When TWC Press printed *The El Paso Salt War*, Director Carl Hertzog and I combed the proofs until we nearly wore them out, and in spite of everything we found a miserable typo on the last page after the book was published. The sentence read, "The War was all wasteful and unnecessary, unless to prove to a pessimist that a man can die bravely in a bad cause." The word "bravely" was spelled "dravely."[7] Carl was speechless but not paralyzed. He printed up a basketful of lowercase *b*'s and pasted them by hand over the offensive *d*'s. Recently I saw a Texana catalogue in which the dealer pointed with pride to the fact that he had one of the copies with the repaired typo on the final page.[8] So the evidence of our shame becomes the triumph of a collector.

One last trait of the Minor Historian is worth noting. His hopeless pursuit of perfection makes him a really charitable and agreeable fellow. Because he is aware of his own shortcomings and inadequacies, he is slow to criticize others. When he reviews a book, he gives all the credit he can and minimizes the weaknesses he sees. When you see a reviewer working over a recent publication with savage irony and gleeful sadism, you know he is not a member of the fraternity. He is the bachelor who knows all about rearing babies. If he had ever published a book himself, he would be more forgiving, though it must be admitted that in some cases when he has half a dozen to his credit, he claims exclusive crowing rights on his dunghill and rejects all attempts to join him.

Even in conversation we Minor Historians learn to be careful as well as kind. Every one of us is full to bursting with his current project and could lecture on it by the hour. We realize, however, that our colleagues are full to bursting also, and conversation between specialists is possible only on a give-and-take basis. A man who charges eagerly into my office with all his pictures and letters and research notes and wants me to spend two hours listening and admiring is obviously an outsider, and I get him out of there as soon as I can. He might be welcome if he would give me equal time. This seldom occurs to him, however, and usually I have an important engagement in ten minutes.

All this may give the idea that a Minor Historian is a solemn, intense, and humorless fellow, but that impression would be wrong. We take our laughs where we find them. They are sometimes wry laughs, because they are at our own expense, but not always.

There was the time, for example, when Carl Hertzog was looking for an original idea to use in book design and decided that he could get a good effect by printing a cover from an adobe building block. The result exceeded his expectations. The straws which held the adobe together were plainly visible.[9] Even flecks of horse manure could be made out. Carl commented that this was the first book he had ever seen in which the manure was on the outside.

So there you have the Minor Historian and his tribe. We are important people in our own way. We do things that need to be done. I do not suggest that a statue of the Minor Historian should replace the figure of Buckey O'Neill in the square at Prescott, Arizona, but I do think we deserve a little recognition. I have long maintained that only when a people knows where it came from can it know where it is going. Only by knowing our past can we look into our future. Only by studying history can we know who we are. The Minor Historians are always busy digging up the little bits of rock which, fitted together, make visible our historical landscape. We help every American know who he is. And we ask no higher praise.

8

Instant History

To HISTORY-MINDED PEOPLE like us it seems strange that many —perhaps most—human beings do not have a sense of history. We expect other people to be like us, and we feel some astonishment when we find that they are not. A hot-rod specialist assumes that all normal males, and most females, are passionate about drag racing. A cowboy finds it strange that you and I find the cow a rather dull subject except in the form of steaks and hamburgers. A historian would like to believe that all intelligent beings share his special interest, but every day we are reminded that they do not.

This sad fact was brought home to me some years ago when I was paying a visit to Dorchester, England, hometown of Thomas Hardy the novelist. Dorchester, as the name indicates (*chester* is derived from the Latin word for a fortified camp), goes back to Roman times, and when I was there, a magnificent Roman villa had just been excavated in the west part of town. I could not get over it. A real Roman villa or gentleman's house (what was left of it) lying there before our eyes! If we had one of those in Texas, I thought, we would cherish and restore it and put a fence around it and charge fifty cents to get in to see it. I said as much to the man at the railroad station where I bought my ticket for London.

"That old thing!" he replied with heavy scorn. "We don't care about it. We are going to cover it up next week and put up a row of modern apartments."

I learned from this and other similar episodes that a sense of history never comes to some people and that most of us have to develop it, like a taste for raw oysters. I learned also that it is likely to come late in life, when we realize that time is passing and our good old days are behind us. The well of human experience is only water until it begins to run dry. Then we sit up and begin to take an interest.

This side of human nature is brought home to us painfully every day. Today we are just waking up to the fact that our pure-water supply is about gone, our pure air is going with it, and our wildlife is vanishing with both. We are told that it is already too late to do anything about it, so everybody is sure that something must be done. We will not stop smoking until one lung is gone and the other is in danger. We will not treat our friends and relatives like human beings until they are packed and ready to leave.

It is the same in literature. Joel Chandler Harris did not think about preserving the songs and saying of Uncle Remus until the old-time Georgia Negro was about to disappear. Bret Harte began painting his portraits of the forty-niners twenty years after the gold rush when the Argonauts were beginning to vanish from the scene. In Texas, Noah Smithwick's daughter put off taking down his reminiscences until he was ninety years old, blind, and close to death. It is really just luck that we now have *The Evolution of a State.*[1]

How many times have you heard someone say, "Grandpa told me a lot about that, but I didn't pay much attention. I wish I had!" How often after a death in the family does a survivor say, "There's no place to put all these papers. I guess we'll just have to burn them." It happens so often that it is almost a rule.

The old courthouse at Tombstone, Arizona, remained unoccupied for some years after the county seat was moved to Bisbee, but eventually a man bought it with the intention of making it into a hotel or rooming house. All the records which had not been moved to Bisbee were in his way, so he rigged a chute from a second-story window to an abandoned mine shaft in the arroyo below and shoveled everything into the hole.

"Well, it must still be down there," I said. "Maybe we could go down and get it."

"No, you can't," they told me. "Somebody else used the mine for a cesspool."

This to me is especially sad because the people who do not care about old records and relics are destroying pieces of their — and our — personalities, part of what we came from. Most of us have many missing parts because the records of our past have been burned or thrown into an abandoned mine shaft or otherwise disposed of, all because somebody did not realize that what he was destroying was history.

Perhaps the classic example of this failure of perception is in a story by John Steinbeck called "The Leader of the People." The viewpoint character is a California boy named Jody Tiflin. His grandfather, way back in the early days, was in charge of a wagon train which crossed the country all the way to the Pacific Coast. Now Grandpa talks about that and nothing else. Everybody is tired of listening to his old stories. His son-in-law says: "He came across the plains. All right! Now it's finished. Nobody wants to hear about it over and over." Grandfather overhears him and is deeply hurt. He begins to think about reasons and motives and says to Jody:

> "It wasn't Indians that were important, nor adventures, nor even getting out there. It was a whole bunch of people made into one big crawling beast. . . . When we saw the mountains at last, we cried — but it wasn't getting there that mattered. It was movement and westering. . . . The westering was as big as God, and the slow steps that made the movement piled up and piled up until the continent was crossed. Then we came down to the sea and it was done." He stopped and wiped his eyes until the rims were red. "That's what I should be telling instead of stories."[2]

Another way of saying it would be that the old man had a sense of history but wasn't getting it across. If Jody had been a Junior Historian, he would have got the old man on tape and gone back two or three times to see whether he could pick up additional details.

All this we know. What we may not realize is that everything we do and say and think is history. What we are looking at is history. What we ate for breakfast this morning is historically significant.

It may be useful to stop here for a moment and remember that some of the best historical sources have been left by people who realized that their day-by-day experiences were important. Think of the young men who joined Doniphan's Expedition in Missouri in 1846 during the Mexican War and came down the Río Grande through New Mexico to El Paso, Mexico, now Juárez. They stayed for several weeks and then went on to Chihuahua to fight the Battle of Sacramento before returning to St. Louis by way of New Orleans. A surprising number of them kept diaries and journals, and anybody who wants to know about Doniphan's Expedition is happy that they did so.[3] They tell us more than a century later what they did and what they ate and how interesting it was to see a pretty Mexican girl riding to church on horseback behind her father or brother or fiancé.[4] How good those El Paso apples and onions tasted! What it was like to camp out in a howling sandstorm! We are lucky to have those diaries. We could not know much about the campaign without them.

The same is true of the Civil War. The accounts left by the participants are what make the history of that time real.[5] Most of them were published long after the events they describe. They lay at the bottom of somebody's old trunk for fifty years, seventy-five years, a hundred years before anybody thought they were worth printing.

Something like this happened not so very long ago to Morris Parker, who came to White Oaks, New Mexico, as a small boy in the early 1880s and grew up in a real, true-life, rip-roaring frontier gold-mining town where Billy the Kid was at home. He told about it in a manuscript that I read half a century ago. I even had some correspondence with Parker, but it never occurred to me — even to me — that I should do anything about his story of White Oaks. It was not a professional job. Who would be interested?

Then one day I paid a call on Harwood Hinton, editor of *Arizona and the West*, with offices on the campus of the University of Arizona at Tucson. He said, "There is one gap I wish we could fill. Nobody has ever done anything on White Oaks, New Mexico. I wish we had something on that."

"We have," I told him. "I have a copy of Morris Parker's manuscript."

In 1971, Morris Parker's story was published in paperback by the University of Arizona Press. I regret very much that Parker could not live to see his book in print, but human nature was against him. There was too much water in the well, and it never occurred to anybody that someday we were going to miss it. Many reminiscent manuscripts were around, along with the men who wrote them. The stories were homemade, inexpertly written — interesting and valuable, of course, but not feasible for commercial publication. No publisher would look at one. The leader of the people was a tiresome old man, and who wanted to listen to his stories?

Now the leaders of the people are all gone. It is too late to talk to them. So their manuscripts are in demand and are getting into print.

I have one myself, written in collaboration with "Aunt Fan" Cochran who grew up in Frio County, south of San Antonio, when the Comanches were still raiding. Bigfoot Wallace lived in her family home off and on for thirty years. She was a one-woman encyclopedia of the pioneer experience, and I took her letters and arranged them to make a book, but no publisher was interested.[6] Aunt Fan is long since gone and is no doubt telling her stories to the inhabitants of another world. Perhaps it is time to try the publishers again.

The conclusion of all this is really the thought that we are living in the good old days this very moment. We are experiencing today what will be history tomorrow, but few of us stop to think that the familiar things we take for granted now will soon vanish from the earth, or at least become rare enough to interest collectors.

All of us who can look back to earlier years in this century think sometimes of how we lived and what we lived with. Ladies wore straitjackets called corsets, and on top of them they had corset covers. They had concoctions of wire and hair called "rats" which they used to deceive the public about the quantity of hair they had. At school we used big, thick, rough-paper tablets called "All You Can Carry." We carried pencil boxes and pencil sharpeners. We chewed Juicy Fruit gum and sucked on hard, round, black-coated balls of candy called jawbreakers that could have doubled for ball bearings. We bought licorice sticks for a penny. Our shoes were fastened with buttons, and we had to have buttonhooks when we put them on. We wore long black stockings, and in winter, when our mothers insisted that we surround ourselves with long underwear, we had lumpy-looking legs. This embarrassed us, especially the girls, and sometimes a young lady who could not stand not to be beautiful defied her mother, put the hateful long underwear back in the dresser drawer, and froze happily almost to death on her way to school. It all seemed so everyday and normal and the way things were that we never thought that what we were doing and saying and eating and wearing was history. But it was. And when anyone stages a play or makes a movie about those times, he has problems. Where can he find any long black stockings and full-length underwear? Does an "All You Can Carry" tablet still exist—or a pencil box or a jawbreaker? Usually such things are very hard to find.

Some years ago the newspapers carried a story about a movie director who wanted to set up a love scene in a buggy. He knew enough about buggies to realize that each one had a whipsocket to hold the buggy whip. He found a buggy, complete with whipsocket, but he could not find a whip. He combed the country, presumably trying even Knotts' Berry Farm in California, and there weren't any. Finally, in a country store in Arkansas, he came across half a dozen buggy whips which had been there since about 1901. He was lucky.

Another newspaper story, some time after midcentury, told about a man in Silver City, New Mexico, who had fallen heir to an original Edison phonograph with two hundred cylinder records. He had a gold mine. Even now it is not unheard of that somebody has discovered a 1923 Buick stashed away in an old barn, complete with rubber-bulb horn and original tires. It is now a classic car and sells for many times what it originally cost. If one does not throw away his old buggy whips or his old hula hoops or his old sheet music or his old records, after a while they become valuable — because they are history.

The hard thing is to get a historic object past the years when it is just old-fashioned junk. The furniture in your house today will be old-fashioned in ten or fifteen years, and your wife will want to trade it in on some real up-to-date pieces. If she would put it up in the attic (assuming she has one) and let it stay there for fifty years, it would make somebody some money. How about that old player piano? It is a collector's item now. How about Grandmother's old home-made "safe" or kitchen cabinet? Museum directors are thrilled to find one. How about your Uncle George's gold toothpick? It is history now, and if nobody is collecting such things at present, he soon will be.

Almost anything is collectible. All survivals are valuable to somebody. Invitations, menus, report cards, hair ornaments, school songs, tools, radio commercials, children's games, horse furniture, slogans — anything is worth saving systematically. A complete collection will someday be unique.

Just one more thing should be added. Pack rats who collect the material, concrete, metal-and-glass-pasteboard relics of the past have an important reason for doing so. Their real object is to know something about the person who used the artifact or sang the song or wore the long black stockings. History, for most of us, is human history. The historical scavenger who spends his Sundays digging in old military posts is triumphant when he finds an empty cartridge or a button, but his interest goes further than the object. Quiz him closely, and you will find that he can tell a good deal about what was going on in the garrison just from the presence of that special type of button. He knows that it was on a jacket or blouse and that the jacket was worn by a soldier. When he looks at the button, he is trying, perhaps without realizing it, to get back to that human being and share his experiences.

Can anyone doubt that this is a good thing for him to do? It makes him less of a self-centered individual and more a member of society. By learning what is behind him, what produced him, he sees more clearly who he is.

And that is what history is for.

9

Dracula in the Stacks

Problems and Perils
of the Small Research Library

A LIBRARIAN'S LIFE is not necessarily a happy one (ask any librarian), but the director of a small research facility faces some special difficulties.[1]

The library of the Arizona Historical Society at Tucson is probably typical with its 50,000 books, 145 periodicals, 72 newspapers, 268,000 photographs, and over 1,000 archival collections—all bearing on the history of Arizona and related areas.[2] The staff consists of nine people, including one archivist and two assistants who work with the photograph collection. Six diligent and dedicated women are charged with meeting the public in the reading room and responding to written requests. It is their sad fate that is discussed here.

The situation is not what they expected when they began their training. As it turns out, their chief concerns are not "Increasing the Library's Resources" and "Making Our Holdings More Readily Available," and the dream of spending long, quiet hours in the world of books remains unrealized. Instead, they have to contend with the human race. Their problems are people problems, and their dilemma is the ancient one—they cannot live comfortably with the public, and they cannot live without it. If there were no people, they would have few problems, but without them, they would have no library.

A few librarians (not the AHS women, of course), try to keep the public out of their little worlds. A story is told of a senior librarian in an Arizona state university who had the tables taken out of the reading room. Her theory was that if students could not sit down to read they would borrow fewer books, thus making her life more serene; and if they did take out books, they would not be around to bother her.

Library users, the people who populate the research librarian's world, fall into four groups. First come the Patrons — the people who make no trouble and are a joy to serve. They are considerate, thoughtful, gracious, undemanding. They are grateful for what is done for them, and they say so; and they never ask that an exception be made in their case or insist on being taken to the head librarian to lodge a complaint. They may be dismissed with a blessing.

The second group — the Pests — are just the opposite. They are inconsiderate, thoughtless, demanding, ungrateful — and noisy. They are the ones who organize small conversational groups in the reading room and react indignantly when they have to be shushed. Some of them are eager to corner the librarian and share their lives with her — tell her all about their projects, their ailments, their family problems, their views on religion and politics. They are time-consuming but seldom a real menace.

The third group — the Pirates — are definitely a menace. They are the ones with razor blades who cut photographs out of early newspapers and remove pages from current magazines. A subdivision of this group carries a battery of felt-tipped pens in assorted colors and is responsible for massive underlining on every page of every book they pick up. Another subdivision, the activist wing, punishes the establishment by walking off with everything that is not fastened down. These bandits can and do steal anything. They are the reason so many librarians have completely lost faith in the human race.

Most lethal of all, without meaning to be, are the Vampires. "The Blood is the Life," said Count Dracula in a communicative moment, and in the library the saying holds true, but it is Time, the blood of the librarian, that is the Life. The Library Vampire, Dracula in the stacks, takes great gulps of it, refreshing himself but leaving his victim exhausted and discombobulated.

Sometimes he is a professional, perhaps a researcher for Time-

Life Books, but usually he is an amateur—a buff—who has become excited about the Old West and wants the librarian to search out, copy, and send him everything she can find about Wyatt Earp or the Apache campaigns in Arizona. "I have heard that Doc Holliday was really married to Big-Nose Kate Elder," he confides. "Can you tell me if this is true?" Since nobody has established the fact that Doc was—or was not—married, the librarian cannot answer the question, but she has to write a letter telling him so, thereby shedding several drops of her time.

Again it is possible to divide the inquirers into special categories. Many of them are children who have been assigned a topic for a paper and need material—right away.

"Dear Gentlemen," writes a young inquisitor from Magna, Utah, on February 6, 1975:

> In my U.S. History class, I have chosen your state Arizona, to do a report on. It would be extremely helpful if you could send me some information on the most important historical events that happened in your state, Arizona. Could you please send the information before October 3, 1975, because my report is due that day.

This one came from Norwalk, Connecticut:

> Gentlemen:
>   I would appreciate it if you would forward to me any free information on Indians, and especially the Crow Indians.
>   If you could forward this at your earliest convenience, I could be most grateful, as I need the information to do a report for school.

The librarian always answers these requests, sometimes with a form letter, explaining that research libraries do not circulate material and that with a limited staff it is impossible to do very much research for anybody, even for students contending with a deadline. If a good reference suggests itself, she passes it on. In so doing, she loses some more blood (time) in or out of the stacks.

Not all students are children and not all the students are writing papers. A college girl taking a course in southwestern history at Redlands University wrote on April 14, 1975, as follows:

In our class the instructor made two statements that I challenge, however, I do not have proof here in California of the facts. His statements were:

1. The Apache Indian tribe surrendered in 1912.
2. Tucson was first called Tubac. Later, the present Tubac in the Santa Cruz valley was established.

I do not desire to embarass [sic] the instructor, but he asked me to bring the source of my information about Tucson and Tubac to class.

In some cases the informational background of the inquirer is so rudimentary that the librarian hardly knows where to begin. An Englishman writes on April 19, 1972:

I wonder if it is possible for you to furnish me with some Historical facts about the Apache Indian tribes in Arizona. The reason for me making this inquirey is mainly because of a book that I've just completed reading titled (Blood Brother). This book was so interesting that I actually became curious to know whether these Indians had become altogether extinct or whether they are still in existence; I would also like to know if these Indians were permanent mountain dwellers and how long had they dwelled in these mountains before the coming of the white man; Is there such a place called Apacheria? and are there mountain regions called dragoons, warm springs etc. . . . Another point that I would like to make if you are able to answer it, and that is was there once a Town called Tomb Stone?

An Englishwoman, equally innocent, announces in a letter to the librarian dated October 18, 1975, that she is coming to the United States—probably to Los Angeles—for a three-week visit. Would she, in that length of time, she inquires,

be able to visit the places of interest mentioned in an illustrated biography by Alexander B. Adams of Geronimo, and is it possible to travel by local transport to those places? It has always been my ambition to visit these places, before say the 1980s, before they vanish.

The librarian did what she could to convince the woman that Skeleton Canyon is not as accessible as Stoke Poges and that Geronimo's haunts in the Sierra Madre of Mexico can hardly be reached at all.

There is always a separate file for lost-mine specialists and treasure hunters of various kinds. In February, 1971, this letter arrived from Salt Lake City:

> I am a grad student of the Univ of Utah doing research work for a paper in the field of history. In this respect I write to you as a last hope to help me get some information I need badly and photos.
>
> In your state, at a place called *Crittenden* in 1891 or 1890 (I think) a remarkable tomb was found in the ground of stone which held a human shaped coffin of a man with long hair down his back like a Chinaman's, a bird atop his head, 6 toes on his right foot, and curious hieroglyphics written on the coffin and/or other articles. My source for this information is the Deseret Weekly of Mar. 14, 1891, pp. 366–367. I need all accounts, works, and photos of this find available. . . . Can I obtain what accounts and pictures there are of this find from you, and if not—from whom then? . . . I wrote to Arizona Univ. there (the wildcats) but they could offer no help. . . . You seem to be about my last hope and I certainly pray you will be able to assist me in this regard.

"I am sorry," the assistant librarian replied, "but there is absolutely nothing in our files pertaining to the find you describe."

The letters keep coming, most of them from people who have read something about lost or hidden gold and are eager to start digging. A man from Denver wrote on January 19, 1975:

> I believe that I have located a large sealed cavern on the Hopi-Navajo Indian Reservation, which contains the tomb of Moctezuma and part of the "Aztec Treasure."
>
> This cavern has not been disturbed. If you are interested, please advise by return mail.

In September the librarian was queried by a resident of Columbus, Ohio, who had read Carlyle and Michaelson's *The Complete Guide to Treasure Hunting:*

In this book they told about a lost lode called "The Lost Belle McKeever Mine." A lode found by a band of Fort Yuma troopers while pursuing a band of Apache Indians who had attacked the McKeever farm and kidnapped Abner McKeever's daughter, Belle, for whom the lode is named. . . . I was hoping you could give me some information regarding this lost lode, or the address of a bureau or persons who can give me any information.

Amateur novelists do not show up in the files as often as treasure hunters, but they do appear — ambitious, enthusiastic, and often completely uninformed. One of them, living in an Arizona retirement community, wrote in 1970 for background information to be used in "my next novel," titled *Every Fourth Night*, which she planned to set on the Empire Ranch southeast of Tucson. The title referred to the sex life of the leading female character. "I cannot find out if the Indians living in the vicinity had any understanding of English or not, and if they had any degree of culture in 'manufacturing' artifacts," she disclosed. "I want to get the actual 'feel' of the Southwest country. . . . Then when it is written, I want to go to Hollywood and have it produced by a writer-producer I know for both T.V. series and cinema."

The librarian did all she could to enlighten this bewildered pilgrim.

Genealogists, particularly the recently awakened, constitute another group with more hope than information:

I'm trying to trace our family history. Someone was an Indian agent & sheriff the way stories are told and someone great or great great was full blooded Apache, would be a woman. . . . Any help or information needed, is greatly appreciated.

Even highly trained technical people have strange requests. A deputy state forester writes early in 1975:

In celebrating the Bicentennial year of American Independence, the American Forestry Association wishes to publish a book on historic and famous trees of the United States. . . . If you are aware of a tree that you would wish to be considered, please submit a photo and pertinent information. . . .

And from a professor and head of a department in a Texas university, this interesting request:

> I am interested in learning whether any journalist in Arizona ever died as a direct consequence of having said or printed statements so offensive to others that they murdered him. . . . I enclose an envelope for your convenience.

Dracula in the stacks is not necessarily native-born. He may be a Frenchman, an Italian, a German, a Norwegian, a Japanese, or an Englishman. Wherever the Old West is known and loved, there will be somebody who wants quantities of information:

> I am a young Norwegian who is very interested in the history of the United States, especially the American West. But it is almost impossible to get hold of books about the persons and the places which have become famous, or about ordinary people, how they lived, how they managed. I would therefore be very glad if I could get some information about these things, about the state itself, and—if it is possible—a list of books concerning the American West which I may buy.

Any American would be sympathetic to a request like this, written in September, 1975, and the librarian does all she can to help. But when a man wants everything, his request cannot be fulfilled.

Without meaning to ask the impossible, researchers in foreign countries place the greatest burden on the staff of the small western research library. About a hundred requests a year come to the AHS librarian. Members of the English Westerners present special problems because they are serious and productive historians who must conduct most of their research operations by remote control and through correspondence. At least one definitive volume, a biography of a famous western peace officer, has been done by an English Westerner who at the time of publication had never visited the United States.[3] All the members are deeply immersed in one project or another and their publications are the product of meticulous investigation. A librarian really wants to help such people but sometimes finds it impossible to answer a blanket request for material:

> I already have the typescript sketch of the history of the 3rd cavalry from the Mrs. Emmett Crawford Norton Collection (*Brandes Guide*, item no. 269) but would like to obtain photocopies of the 150 telegrams sent from Camp Thomas to San Carlos in 1884.

The 150 telegrams were only a small part of the material needed by this correspondent, and when the librarian explained that with her limited staff she could provide only a fraction of what he wanted, he was deeply hurt and disappointed. He obtained the name of the assistant librarian and registered his complaint with her:

> Regrettably I was never able to establish with [the librarian] the cordial relationship that I have with the various other persons with whom I have, and do, exchange correspondence upon the subject of the Apache campaigns. . . . Unfortunately I was able to elicit only three letters from that lady over a period from June, 1970, to September, 1971. . . . This was something of a bitter pill as the Arizona Historical Society collections represent one of the major archival sources for a researcher with my particular interests but the only means of continuing appeared to be to make some sort of formal complaint and that I considered a rather unsavoury course to have to resort to.

The assistant librarian, placed in an embarrassing position by this letter, wisely turned it over to the director of the Arizona Historical Society, who explained the situation clearly to the disgruntled Englishman:

> There are now enormous demands on our small library staff. Last year we responded to 8,000 research inquiries with a library staff of four people serving a reading room full of researchers every day as well as those who write to us. . . . In our case, first priority is given to Arizona students and researchers and among those, first priority is given to those who are actually physically using our resources. Obviously time and distance make it impossible for you to be here but unfortunately lengthy and time-consuming requests such as yours

make it difficult to answer in any reasonable length of time. [The librarian] in fact has extended to you certainly more than average service under our present operating circumstances. . . . I hope these points have clarified our operating conditions here and that you will understand why it will be impossible for us to satisfy a request as involved as yours at one time and in short order. If you would like to select those items for copy that you most urgently need, we will do the best we can.

The file of indignant letters gets thicker every year, but perhaps the best example came from a student living in Peoria, Illinois, dated March 25, 1972:

Gentlemen:
This letter pertains to your library department. I was under the false impression that your state's historical society would willingly cooperate with someone who is trying to write a paper about one of your former inhabitants, namely Wyatt Earp. In my school and city libraries there is very little truthful information about this man so naturally I felt that you people would help me. However, this was a wrong assumption. I *wasted* approximately $7.00 talking long distance to your library department and it was to no avail.
Your library department told me to use library loan to get several books, so the Peoria Public Library ordered these books from your library. Instead of replying promptly that you couldn't loan your precious, valuable books, your librarians wasted two weeks. This was not only rude, but also inconsiderate. I depended on you and you let me down!! Because of this, my term paper grade will suffer drastically. . . . If this behavior is an example of how other institutions in the glorious (hah!) state of Arizona are run, I am honestly glad that I will have no further contact with you or any other inhabitants of your state.

That is the way things go in a small research library. A casual visitor could hardly guess that the pleasant, helpful person behind the desk in the reading room of the Arizona Historical Society is in such peril and that there is no escape. If she takes a vacation (which even Vampires regard as an inalienable human right), she returns to a desk piled high with pleas for help. She was behind when she left, anemic from so much time letting, and now she is behinder. Facing a feverish future with her usual courage, however, she picks up the first letter, addressed to "Dear Sirs":

> I am in the 4th grade of Arredondo School. We are doing reports on a subject about Arizona. I have chosen Carl Hayden. Would you please send me any pamphlets, pictures or information? I need it soon. Thank you for your help.

10

The Editor — A Necessary Evil

IN THE HISTORY BUSINESS one indispensable individual is often overlooked, downgraded, even resented — the editor of a state, local, or regional quarterly. The common persuasion that he is an autocratic, undereducated, fussy, demanding, opinionated egoist is all wrong. He is really a much-burdened helpful person who is often taken advantage of — a humble workman to whom Sam Johnson's definition of a lexicographer would apply: a harmless drudge.

The historian, indeed, could hardly do without him. He is, for all his lowly estate, the Saint Peter of the profession, guarding the gates of Paradise — that is, publication. Many a fledgling practitioner would never make it without him, for he can and does make sense out of the unreadable and polishes up the unpublishable. Even the Great Guns of historical scholarship need him, for no human being who takes typewriter in hand can see all the way around what he writes. A disinterested observer who knows his business — that is, an editor — can always find a better word, cut across a circumlocution, catch a discrepancy, improve a transition. When the disinterested observer himself takes typewriter in hand, it should be added, he needs another disinterested observer to check him out. Even an editor needs an editor.

They come in all shapes and sizes, and no two are alike, a fact which helps to explain the wide variety of historical magazines — all the way from *True West* to the *American Historical Review*. The harmless drudge, however, is somewhere between the two extremes. The editor of a state, city or regional journal, for instance the *Journal of Arizona History* (published at Tucson by the Arizona Historical Society) is a fair example.[1] With the help of an assistant editor, an editorial assistant, a modest state subsidy, and a percentage of the dues paid annually by about 3,500 bona fide AHS members, he turns out a handsome magazine and publishes two to five books a year. He is not without dignity and is certainly useful, but he is far below the salt at the table where the editor of the *American Historical Review* sits in majesty with throngs of business managers and assistant editors to do his bidding, dozens of reviewers and digesters of articles laboring in his salt mine, a corps of readers working steadily through heaps of submitted manuscripts, and a battery of graduate students checking references. The products are lined up like Christmas turkeys in a packing plant and are published in order of acceptance.[2] This is the historical Big Time. The *Arizona Historical Quarterly* is not in the same league, and neither is its editor.

The regional journal is different, for one thing, because of its special audience. Scholars use it, but it is produced for the members of the Arizona Historical Society. They include a small percentage of little old ladies in sneakers and an equally small percentage of professional historians, academic or otherwise; but most of the readers are somewhere between the uninitiated and the sophisticated. The old rhyme fits them: doctor, lawyer, merchant, chief. They are history buffs — amateurs — but in their own way they are scholars. They know a great deal of local history; they want the truth; they do not settle for popular rehashes or once-over-lightly journalism. They are hard to fool, and they object strenuously to slipshod research, so the magazine must be, in the best sense, scholarly. The typical article must be carefully researched and thoroughly documented.

At the same time these nonprofessionals ask for something besides dry husks of scholarship. They are not usually researching anything, and they do not have to wade through muddy writing and confusing organization. They would like to be interested — even amused — as well as informed, and the Small Editor, the editor of the small magazine, does his best to satisfy them. The historian who wants to, or has to, write for such a journal had better keep them in mind too.

Here again the Small Editor differs from the Big Editor since he works with a different kind of material. The Big Editor asks that the articles he accepts be clearly and concisely written and efficiently organized, but they need not be bright or lively. In fact, they had better not be. As a result these weighty contributions can seldom be "read." Rather, they are consulted and used by specialists. Their ultimate fate is to be bound and filed on library shelves. "Laid away" might be a better term.

The small regional journal cannot afford to sell its periodical soul in this manner. It has to avoid essays which will be of interest only to narrow specialists. Military history, for example is staple fare. In Arizona the Apache campaigns, frontier forts, the Civil War, the Mexican Revolution–all are of interest to the target reader. But the editor shies away from papers on "Horseshoes Discovered in Excavations at Old Fort Grant" or "Utilization of the Abandoned Bed of the Salt River Inside the City Limits of Phoenix." A good rule of thumb is to look for articles which concentrate on people. Statistics may endure for a night, but human history cometh in the morning.

An occasional reminiscent article helps–the recollections of someone who was there when it happened. The archives of any historical society are full of these first-person accounts. Naturally they are not documented and are not, in the strictest sense, "scholarly." One would not expect the Big Editor to use them, but the Small Editor can make points with his public if he includes one now and then. He is aware that some of his readers begin at the beginning of his journal but that a surprising number begin at the end and work backward, so the right position for one of these hors d'oeuvres ("tidbits," one editor calls them) is either first or last. This would be heresy for the Big Editor, who likes to start with a "lead article"–usually the longest and dullest in that issue.

To give the browsers something tasty at the halfway point, some journals, including the *Journal of Arizona History*, offer a photographic essay with text and pictures—on man's best friend the burro; on early aviation in Arizona; on early-day bicycle clubs; on the building of Roosevelt Dam, which made Greater Phoenix possible; on mining camps and Indian reservations.[3] The picture story is one of the best ways of teaching regional history, but its use is pretty much limited to the regional magazines.

The editor, of course, must resist temptation to concede too much to the "popular." Material about gunfighters and fancy women, always appealing to a certain kind of reader, is acceptable if there is new information, but he would never, no, never, print an essay beginning: "It was Saturday night in Tombstone and hell was threatening to break loose. Marshal Earp stalked down the middle of Allen Street, his Winchester in the crook of his elbow, his keen eyes darting right and left as he searched for trouble-makers in the noisy throng." This sort of thing obviously would not do, but somewhere between the popular and the pedantic is the proper middle ground, and if the editor is good at his job, he finds it.

Along with its nonprofessional audience and its less formal and less specialized material, the small quarterly differs from the big one in still anther way—the kinds of contributors it attracts. These include local historians with tremendous enthusiams but very little writing experience, graduate students eager to get something into print, and sometimes a professor with a piece which has been turned down by all the better journals. Not many of the amateurs are able to produce really publishable material, and some truly atrocious copy comes to the editor's desk. The professors are often just about as bad. They overestimate themselves as writers, need more help than they realize, and view with deep suspicion or outright resentment any attempt to upgrade their work. The fine points of English are of secondary importance in their universe. They do not know about hyphenating compound adjectives before the noun. They misspell. They are guilty of endless verbal repetition. They do not know the difference between "disinterested" and "uninterested." They think a "cohort" is a sidekick or companion—not the tenth part of a Roman legion. And since these professors may not recognize finished writing when they see it—or its opposite—their students may apply even more rudimentary skills.

A professor I once knew was indignant when an editor told him his style was angular and his writing was dull.

"I don't care about that," he protested. "My structure is sound, my statements are documented and my conclusions are justified. What more do you want? Why worry about the paint job?"

"I agree that a solid structure is the first requirement," replied the editor, "but without a good paint job, you can't sell your building."

Strangely enough the hardest people to deal with in this department are contributors with newspaper experience. Perhaps because they have to work fast—perhaps because they rely on a copy editor to give their newspaper stories a final going over—they seldom turn in finished copy. They use rough paper, strike over letters, x-out lines, and give a minimum of attention to their references. They never did believe much in footnotes anyway, doubting that anybody ever looks at them, and they seldom consult the journal to familiarize themselves with its reference style. The editor is always trying to find volume numbers, identify place of publication, or determine whether the title is a book, an article, or a manuscript. He knows he is a drudge as he goes about these chores.

The Big Editor can send an unsatisfactory article back for revision or reject it outright. The Small Editor tries to salvage an essay if it has any possibilities at all. This brings up the fourth way in which the small periodical differs from the great ones: the editor rewrites, or at least rearranges, almost everything he uses. He believes there is no other way to deal with the situation. He knows the writer of an unsatisfactory article has already done all he knows how to do and that if the piece is to be salvaged the editor himself will have to make the necessary repairs.

Suppose he has on his desk an essay forty pages long on early copper mining in central Arizona. He could send it back to the author with instructions to cut it to twenty-five pages. The author replies:

"This piece was seventy-five pages long when I wrote it. I have already cut it and I can't cut it any more."

There is no point in telling this man that any subject can be treated at any length, so the editor cuts it for him.

It is the same with stylistic matters.

"You have too many paragraphs" (speaking to a newspaperman).

"That is the way I learned to do it. I can't change now."

"Your sentences are awkward."

"How? They sound all right to me."

"You are not saying what you mean."

"It is perfectly clear to me."

So the question has to be answered: Is it better to have an acceptably written magazine with the editor doing the remodeling or leave the essays in their virgin state, untouched by civilization? The Small Editor feels that he has little or no choice. He has to use what is available and make it publishable, remembering always the first rule of historical editing: You may improve the style but you must not change the meaning. And when the author thinks his meaning has been altered or obscured, it is the editor's business to work with him until both are satisfied.

That is why the Small Editor is a harmless drudge. Improving other people's prose is like charity done in secret. It is gratifying to see the results, but being an anonymous donor can become boring.

The situation would be bearable if it were not for the human tendency to dislike a benefactor. Sooner or later the editor's anonymous donations will get him in trouble. If he is diplomatic and consults his contributors on every point, yielding as much as he can and trying to see the writer's point of view, the evil day may be long postponed, but eventually there will be thunder in the air and perhaps rain and hail. It will not come from the graduate students. They are so happy to be published that no price is too high. Nor will it come from seasoned writers. When an old pro submits an article, he is well aware that nobody's words are sacred, especially after the article is in page proofs, and he usually tells the editor to go ahead and do what is necessary about cutting or expanding or changing a word to make the letter count come out right. There is no peril from these contributors. It is the man who has published an article or two and has begun to think of himself as a writer who wants no word changed and raises the whirlwind if he is not allowed to speak in his own semiliterate way.

The editor of the *Journal of Arizona History* ran into trouble when he was dealing with an article by a retired colonel on the history of an early-day military encampment in southeastern Arizona. The story focused on a dashing lieutenant who was drowned while crossing a swollen mountain river. The editor felt that the colonel needed to do more homework, and when results were slow to appear, the editorial staff undertook to do a little supplementary research themselves. They found almost at once that the unfortunate lieutenant had very important connections – was, in fact, a brother-in-law of General Philip Sheridan. This added some new dimensions to the account, and they so reported to the author. He did not believe them – thought they were fictionizing.

"You may publish your fantasies in *True West*," he wrote indignantly. "I won't have my name on them."

Fortunately the editors were able to convince him that they were right. He dug deeper and turned out a successful and – with their help – readable article.[4] He has been their firm friend ever since.

The same could not be said of a later contributor, an important lawyer from another part of the country who was spending his winters in Arizona. He turned in a less-than-satisfactory article which the staff undertook to improve. They rearranged his material, ran down references, secured photographs from points far away, and polished his prose, being careful to consult him on every point and finding him entirely reasonable until the journal was mailed out. Then he wrote a letter beginning: "I sure want to thank you for sending me those copies of that piece. I enjoyed reading it although I didn't know it was mine, the way you wrote it, until I saw my name on it. It was better the way I had it."

Shocked and dismayed, the editors framed the letter and displayed it thenceforth to brothers of the craft as a contribution to the Bite-the-Hand-that-Feeds-You Department.

The harmless drudge knows that such protests are inevitable. He forgives the protesters and continues to do what he must. He knows that a good beginning is important, so he takes a paragraph from page three and uses it for a leadoff, saving the writer's ponderous introductory paragraphs, or part of them, for a conclusion. He will rearrange pages to make sure that ideas belonging together are all in one place. He may drop in a few words to build a bridge between two divisions and point out a new direction. The result is almost entirely in the author's own words, but pace and tension are improved, a recognizable thesis or objective emerges, and the reader's comprehension and convenience are considered.

Most contributors are grateful for the help they get and pleased with the result. They may even feel that they have learned something they need to know.

It is clear that the editor is what the title calls him and that, God helping him, he can be no other. The catalogue of his pains and perils, however, is not complete, and it would be good for his readers and contributors to hear about them.

First, like Robinson Crusoe he is alone on his desert island. He works in isolation and without much human contact. One might compare him to Walt Whitman's noiseless, patient spider "sending out filament, filament, filament" hoping one of them will "catch somewhere."[5] A still better analogy would compare him with a man in a prison cell tapping out messages on the water pipes for listeners who may or may not exist.

Every three months the journal goes out to its 3,500 members, but the only response the editor can expect is from people who are offended or catch him in a mistake. Suppose, for example, he runs a piece on the Bisbee Deportations of 1917 in which over 1,100 striking miners were loaded on cattle cars by several hundred deputy sheriffs and company men and deposited in the middle of the New Mexico desert.[6] The author is a young liberal who is obviously on the side of the striking miners. Inevitably a letter arrives from a conservative senior citizen who believes that the strikers were in the pay of the German government in time of war and were traitors to their country. "You have done irreparable harm," he says.

Less important matters draw fire. If mention is made of Buckey O'Neill, the famous peace officer and Rough Rider, and his name is spelled O'Neal, he will hear from three or four subscribers some of whom do not know that O'Neill spelled his nickname "Buckey" and not "Bucky."

Sometimes the author of a book which has been reviewed will write to protest what he considers an injustice. But if anyone approves of the magazine, he usually keeps his feelings to himself. The Small Editor has to be satisfied with knowing—or hoping—that the work of his hands is good, useful, and readable.

On the plus side he emerges from his ordeal humbled and chastened, a better man. He even has new insights into literature. He comes to believe that Shakespeare must have had some experience as an editor, for he says, "The evil that men do lives after them." Likewise he learns to claim certain verses in the Bible as his own: "Let him who thinketh he standeth take heed lest he fall"; and the editor's special one, "Speak not with a stiff neck and set not up your horn on high, for behold, promotion cometh neither from the east nor from the west."

The young scholar who comes to realize these things—and the old scholar too—may well purge his heart of scorn and resentment, accept the editor's aid with good grace, and forgive him for what may seem high-handed tactics and picayune criticism. The harmless drudge, laboring night and day to accomplish the impossible, deserves tolerance if not praise and should be regarded as, at worst, a necessary evil.

11

The Fine Art of Plagiarism

THE HISTORIAN'S LIFE, like that of most other human beings, arranges itself in a sort of standard pattern. Basically this pattern is a circle. It begins with the pursuit of truth, which is said to be the scholar's primary objective. As a teacher and writer he disseminates truth, which he has pursued and presumably caught. His students and readers absorb it, digest it, and use it as a means of arriving at new insights. These, in turn, become available to the original scholar and make it possible for him to start the cycle over again. The circle is by no means a vicious one. The historian's existence could be simple and satisfying, and it would be if administrators were kinder and if scholars did not disagree so furiously and make existence hard for each other. Sometimes, however, people in patterns should stop and ask if the rules they live by make sense. Quite often they do not.

This applies to the historian. As a man in pursuit of truth, his activities fall under the general head of research. Research involves the use of source material—records of all kinds, primary and secondary, written and oral. The soundness of his conclusions is vouched for by exact references to his basic documents.

The difficulty is that this source material comes from other people—people who have recorded it, accumulated it, or lived it. The fundamental idea here is a good one. The pooling of information should bring the researcher nearer to the truth, and mostly it does, but the nature of man sometimes gets in the way. The human mind is a peculiar thing, opinionated, myopic, prejudiced, subject to delusion and error, and this complicates the historian's task.

Take, for instance, the case of a professor in a southwestern university, a good scholar and teacher, who specializes in Methods of Research and Bibliography. He begins his lectures by asking his students to answer the question: "What is a fact?" When enough time has been spent in groping for an answer, he reveals that for a scholar a fact is a statement or idea which can be supported by a reference to a reliable source. That is, nothing is true unless somebody says it is.

The weakness in this method of pursuing truth is evident when one admits, as he must, that the source is a human being who may be mistaken or misled, in which case the reference merely perpetuates error. Historians realize this, usually early in their careers, when they observe that once a mistaken idea gets into print, it takes on a life of its own, is cited over and over by students who do not bother to check it out, and reduces to despair the people who have the correct information. The romanticizing of the western gunman provides many examples. Wyatt Earp in *Frontier Marshal* has passed into folklore, and Stuart Lake's inventions will probably never be eradicated by serious researchers. Thus complete and undiscriminating reliance on source material is one absurdity to which researchers may fall prey.

Another is the notion that unless a book is footnoted it cannot be scholarly. The rule is justified when historical narrative is involved, but suppose a writer wants to do some original thinking about history as an art or business. He cannot very well footnote his own thoughts, but unless his thoughts are footnoted, he may have difficulty finding a publisher.

This is not just theory. A preliminary version of this volume, undocumented and unblessed, was declined by two university presses because, by the terms of their charters, they were limited to the publication of "scholarly" — that is footnoted — books. One director said in his letter of rejection:

As a scholarly publisher, we are regarded as an "actual-factual" publisher. Further, in a state of our size, publications carrying its name are regarded as expressing the views and stands of the university. . . . Accordingly, we pretty much do restrict ourselves to "this is how it is," as opposed to individual expressions of "this is how it seemed to me it is."

Some interesting speculations are set in motion by such a statement. The present chapter, of course, is not "scholarly" because it expresses the author's opinion and is not based on other people's opinions. But supposing a historian should find something in it worth quoting. Would it become scholarly because somebody quoted it? Would quotation make it true?

If one pursues this sort of thinking, the Groves of Academe begin to look like a jungle.

The going becomes even rougher when we concentrate on the idea that research often relies on source material recorded or assembled by other men. In other words, scholars pick other people's brains, and scholarship could just as easily be called scavenging, shoplifting, or just plain theft. The word we use is "documentation." This means that if you lift another man's thought or language it is all right if you admit that you lifted it.

Here again we have a set of rules. Almost all taboos can be broken if one follows the proper procedure. The Ten Commandments admonish us, "Thou shalt not covet." But it is permitted if you have a mortgage. Again, "Thou shalt not bear false witness." But if you run an advertising agency, it is expected of you. It is called "creating a demand." In the business of productive scholarship, brain picking is likewise legitimate if done according to rule. I distinguish six of these guiding principles:

1. *Think Big.* Success and respectability depend on the amount of brain picking you do. If you get all your information from one book, you are a plagiarist and can expect to be sued. If you use material from fifty books, you are a scholar and worthy of respect. If you quote from a hundred, you are an authority and may hope to be reviewed in the *New York Times.*

2. *Be Bold.* This is where the documentation comes in. You admit in your notes that you got your "facts" from somebody else. The more notes, the better your scholarship. Great scholars some-

times have more notes than text. Possibly the ideal situation would be all notes and no text at all.

3. *Be Cautious.* Remember that custom permits quotations of fifty words or less in reviews and scholarly works without asking permission of author or publisher, but if you put the ideas in your own words, you can claim them for your very own. You can be sued for verbal borrowings but almost never for borrowing ideas.

4. *Be Thorough.* The Supreme Sin is to overlook something. Other scholars are alert for any indication that you have missed a key source, and they will slay you if they catch you. A good thief— that is a good researcher—gets it all.

5. *Remember Where You Got It.* I once heard of a professor who got up his lectures and delivered them unchanged for years. He eventually came to believe that they had been given to him as the Ten Commandments were given to Moses. When he retired, he decided to put his material into a book and was immediately taken to court for plagiarism.

6. *Be Dull.* All scholars react violently against any lightness of touch, any use of the imagination, any play of fancy or wit. Scholarship, unless it is produced by a Frenchman or an Englishman, must be boring, just as medicine must taste bad and virtue must be painful.

These paragraphs should make it clear that documentation is not the only way of getting at the truth. The *reductio ad absurdum,* the tool used in the paragraphs above, sometimes offers a better way. The obvious fact here is that scholars live by assumptions which they seldom examine critically.

A man identifies himself by his behavior when it is pointed out to him that he is living in a pattern that does not always make sense. A pedant shakes his fist and growls, "Nonsense!" when one of his sacred oxen is gored. A humane scholar smiles at his own absurdities and reflects, as a convicted plagiarist goes by, "There but for the grace of God go I."

Notes

CHAPTER 1

1. Oscar Handlin, *Truth in History*, p. 3.
2. *Ibid.*, pp. viii, 6, 8, 17, 20, 71, 79, 164, 196ff., 410-11.
3. *Ibid.*, p. 158.
4. *Ibid.*, pp. 414-15.
5. Peter M. Stearns and Josel A. Tarr, "Born Again Historians Stepping out of Academic Closet," *Arizona Daily Star*, June 17, 1980.
6. *Ibid.*
7. James A. Henretta, "Social History as Lived and Written," *American Historical Review*, vol. 84 (December, 1979), p. 1293.
8. *Ibid.*, pp. 1310-11.
9. Handlin, *Truth in History*, pp. 58, 119, 122, 128, 134.
10. *Ibid.*, p. 405.

CHAPTER 2

1. Alexander Pope, "An Essay on Criticism," *Pope's Poetical Works*, ed. Herbert Davis, p. 72, lines 97-98.
2. Arnold Bergstrasser, *Goethe's Image of Man and Society*, p. 62, discusses Goethe's view of the role of emotion.
3. Elizabeth Sewell, *Human Metaphor*, p. 47; James Reeves, *Understanding Poetry*, pp. 168-72.
4. Thomas Wolfe, *The Face of a Nation: Poetical Passages from the Writings of Thomas Wolfe*.
5. Una Pope-Hennessey, *Charles Dickens*, p. 149, quotes R. H. Horne's rearrangement of passages from Dickens to resemble blank verse.
6. William Wordsworth, "Ode on the Intimations of Immortality," *Oxford Anthology of English Poetry*, ed. Howard Foster Lowry, pp. 651-52.
7. Eugene Manlove Rhodes, *Best Novels and Stories*, ed. Frank V. Dearing, p. 462.
8. Ralph Waldo Emerson, "The American Scholar," in *Nature Addresses and Lectures*, p. 86.

9. J. R. R. Tolkien, *Beowulf, the Monsters and the Critics*, Sir Israel Gollancz Memorial Lecture, British Academy, 1936.

10. Sir Philip Sidney, *Sidney's Apologie for Poetry*, ed. J. Churton Collins, pp. 4, 12.

11. Percy Bysshe Shelley, "Shelley's Defense of Poetry," in *The Four Ages of Poetry*, Percy Reprints no. 3 (Oxford: Basil Blackwell, 1921), p. 31.

12. Thomas Babington Macaulay, *Critical and Historical Essays*, arranged by A. J. Greene, vol. 1, p. 1.

13. Arthur M. Schlesinger, Jr., *The Age of Jackson*, p. 3.

14. *Ibid.*, p. 89.

15. Ralph Waldo Emerson, "The Poet," in *Essays, Second Series*, pp. 40-41.

16. Sir Philip Sidney, *The Miscellaneous Works of Sir Philip Sidney, Knt.*, ed. William Gray, p. 127.

CHAPTER 3

1. Savoie Lottinville, *The Rhetoric of History*, p. 28.

2. Charles Dickens, *Martin Chuzzlewit*, p. 258.

3. Charles Pilpel, "Rehabilitation," *Harper's*, vol. 250 (January, 1975), pp. 8-9.

4. *Journal of Popular Culture*, vol. 8 (Summer, 1974), pp. 28-34.

5. *Ibid.*, pp. 132-53.

6. *Western American Literature*, vol. 10 (August, 1975), p. 107.

7. Jane Barry, *A Time in the Sun*, p. 105.

8. Joseph Arpad, "The Relations of Folklore and Popular Culture Studies," MS (Paper read at the 1975 meeting of the American Folklore Society).

CHAPTER 4

1. Austin G. Olney, editor-in-chief, Trade Division, Houghton Mifflin Co., in a letter to *Time* (vol. 113 [March 19, 1979], pp. 7-8), revealed that he receives manuscripts every year from "3,000 or so hopeful authors" and accepts "perhaps two or three."

2. Chuck Ross, "Rejected," *New West*, vol. 4 (February 12, 1979), pp. 34-43.

3. Publisher's editor, interview with C. L. S., Tulsa, Oklahoma, October 9, 1975.

4. Richard F. Snow, associate editor, *American Heritage*, to C. L. S., May 16, 1975.

5. "Jonathan Gillam and the White Man's Burden," *Persimmon Hill*, vol. 6 (Winter, 1974), pp. 52–57.

6. Western Writers of America, *Spurs*, pp. 456–68.

7. Savoie Lottinville, *The Rhetoric of History*, p. 28.

8. *Suntracks* is an anthology, issued yearly, of work produced by Indian students in the University of Arizona. Professor of English Lawrence Evers heads the faculty committee in charge.

9. Carobeth Laird, *Encounter with an Angry God*.

10. Wallace Stegner, *The Uneasy Chair: A Biography of Bernard De Voto* (Garden City: Doubleday, 1974), pp. 443–44. Cameron retired in 1979 (*Publishers Weekly*, March 5, 1979).

11. Helen Baldock Craig, *Within Adobe Walls*.

12. *Book Talk*, vol. 8 (June, 1979), p. 4.

13. Marjorie C. Skillin and Robert M. Gay, *Words into Type*, 3d ed.

14. Henderson's *Publish-It-Yourself Handbook* (1979), first issued by Pushcart Press in 1973, is available from Dustbooks, P.O. 1056, Paradise, CA 95969. Chickadel's *Publish It Yourself* is issued by Trinity Press, Box 1320, San Francisco, CA 94101. The Ross *Encyclopedia of Self-Publishing*, published in 1979, comes from Communication Creativity, 5644 La Jolla Blvd., La Jolla, CA 92037. Poynter's *Self-Publishing Manual* was issued in 1979 by Parachuting Publications, Santa Barbara, CA 93103.

15. *Publishers Weekly*, vol. 214 (August 21, 1978), p. 27.

16. Winter Griffith, interview with C. L. S., Tucson, January 4, 1980.

17. Creative Press, Box 9292, College Station, TX 77840.

18. Book Talk, 8632 Horacio Place, N.E., Albuquerque, NM 87111.

19. Books of the Southwest, University Library, University of Arizona, Tucson, AZ 85721.

20. Dustbooks, P.O. Box 1056, Paradise, CA 95969, WIP, Box 31249, San Francisco, CA 94131.

21. *Publishers Weekly*, vol. 218 (July 4, 1980), p. 71.

22. *Ibid.*, November 18, 1980, p. 28.

23. Jelm Mountain Publications, 304 South 3d, Laramie, WY 82070.

24. *Publishers Weekly*, vol. 217 (May 30, 1980), p. 62.

25. Creative Options, P.O. Box 601. Edmonds, WA 98020.

CHAPTER 6

1. Louis L'Amour, *The Lonely Men*, p. 14.
2. "Some Unpublished History of the Southwest: An Old Diary Found in Mexico," chapter 9 (continued), by Mrs. Granville Oury, annotated by Colonel C. C. Smith, U.S. Army, Ret., *Arizona Historical Review*, vol. 6 (January, 1935), p. 61; J. Ross Browne, *Adventures in the Apache Country: A Tour Through Arizona and Sonora.*
3. Arizona Pioneers Historical Society Register, 1888–1895, Arizona Historical Society, Tucson, p. 390 (Poston's call); "The Pioneers," *Tucson Daily Citizen*, February 1, 1884 (account of the proceedings); *Arizona State Historical Society*, ed. Odie B. Faulk (Tucson: Arizona Pioneers Historical Society, 1966), pp. 1–5.
4. *Arizona State Historical Society*, p. 2.
5. *Ibid.*, p. 1; "Certificate of Incorporation of Society of Arizona Pioneers," *Institution and Incorporation*, Arizona Historical Society, p. 1, AHS.
6. *Ibid.*, p. 3.
7. *Ibid.*, p. 4, art. 18.
8. Arizona Pioneers Historical Society Minute Book No. 1, p. 49, AHS.
9. Don Schellie, *Vast Domain of Blood*, p. 125.
10. *Condition of the Indian Tribes: Report of the Joint Special Committee Appointed Under the Joint Resolution of March 3, 1865.*
11. Adolph A. Bandelier, *The Delight Makers*; Marah Ellis Ryan, *Indian Love Letters.*
12. Harold Bell Wright, *The Mine with the Iron Door.*
13. Edgar Rice Burroughs, *Apache Devil.*
14. Elliott Arnold, *Blood Brother.*
15. Jane Barry, *A Time in the Sun.*
16. Dee Brown, *Bury My Heart at Wounded Knee*, p. xiii.
17. *Black Elk Speaks: Being the Life Story of a Holy Man of the Oglala Sioux, as Told Through John G. Neihardt*, p. 9.
18. Quoted in Stan Steiner, *The Vanishing White Man*, p. 123.
19. Wilbur Jacobs, *Dispossessing the American Indian*; Wendell H. Oswaldt, *This Land Was Theirs: A Study of the American Indian.*
20. Nasnaga, *Indians' Summer.*
21. Mabel Dodge Luhan, *Edge of Taos Desert*, p. 295.

22. Vine Deloria, Jr., *God Is Red*, pp. 62, 64-65, 69, 294.

23. Steiner, *The Vanishing White Man*, p. 123.

24. John Upton Terrell, *Apache Chronicle*, pp. xii-xv.

25. Francis P. Brady, "Portrait of a Pioneer," *Journal of Arizona History*, vol. 16 (Summer, 1975), pp. 171-91.

26. Cornelius C. Smith, Jr., *William Sanders Oury: History Maker of the Southwest*, pp. 2-13.

27. Typescript, copy in William Sanders Oury File, AHS.

28. Randy Kane, "An Honorable and Upright Man," *Journal of Arizona History*, vol. 19 (Summer, 1978), p. 305.

29. Farrington Carpenter, interview, Hayden, Colorado, April 28, 1949.

30. Walter Prescott Webb, *The Great Frontier*.

31. Tom Cannon, interview, El Paso, Texas, February 26, 1946.

32. William Sanders Oury, "Speech Made at the Completion of the S.P.R.R., Tucson, March 20, 1880," W. S. Oury file, AHS.

CHAPTER 7

1. Arthur Miller, *Death of a Salesman*, p. 138.

2. C. L. Sonnichsen, *The Mescalero Apaches*.

3. For example, Colin Rickards, *Bowler Hats and Stetsons: Stories of Englishmen in the Wild West*; Joseph G. Rosa and Robin May, *Gunsmoke: A Study of Violence in the Wild West*; Allan Radbourne, "The Naming of Mickey Free," *Journal of Arizona History*, vol. 17 (Autumn, 1976), pp. 341-46.

4. Postcard signed by "Edison Bugbane" and postmarked November 4, 1944, at Brinkley, Arkansas.

5. C. L. Sonnichsen, *Pass of the North: Four Centuries on the Río Grande*, "The El Paso Police Department," following p. 371, caption: J. H. Darose (Daross).

6. F. V. Morley, ed., *Everybody's Boswell*, p. 97.

7. C. L. Sonnichsen, *The El Paso Salt War*, p. 61.

8. Alcazar Book Service, P.O. Box 12764, El Paso, TX, catalogue no. 156, Winter-Spring, 1978-79, p. 18: "This item contains the famous repair work by Carl Hertzog, who went over each copy to replace one letter by hand."

9. Hertzog used the adobe block several times as a cover design. See Joseph M. Ray, *On Becoming a University: Report on an Octennium*.

CHAPTER 8

1. Noah Smithwick, *The Revolution of a State; or Recollections of Old Texas Days.*

2. John Steinbeck, "The Leader of the People," in *The Golden Argosy: A Collection of the Most Celebrated Stories in the English Language,* ed. Van H. Cartmell and Charles Grayson, p. 540.

3. For example, M. B. Edwards's "Journal," in Ralph P. Bieber, *Marching with the Army of the West;* and George Rutledge Gibson, *Journal of a Soldier Under Kearny and Doniphan, 1846-1847,* ed. Ralph P. Bieber.

4. Philip Gooch Ferguson, "Diary of Philip Gooch Ferguson," in Bieber, *Marching with the Army of the West,* p. 348.

5. See Bell Irvin Wiley, *The Life of Johnny Reb, the Common Soldier of the Confederacy.*

6. Frances Bramlette Farris and C. L. Sonnichsen, "South of the Alamo," MS.

CHAPTER 9

1. This chapter was prepared with the assistance of Margaret Bretharte, librarian, and Lori Davisson, research specialist, of the Arizona Historical Society.

2. Collection of documentary material began with the founding of the Arizona Pioneers Historical Society (now the Arizona Historical Society) in 1884.

3. For example, Joseph G. Rosa, author of the definitive life of Wild Bill Hickok, *They Called Him Wild Bill: The Life and Adventure of James Butler Hickok.* Rosa now visits the United States every year.

CHAPTER 10

1. The *Journal of Arizona History* began publication in 1961 as *Arizonian.* The name was changed in 1965.

2. Martin Ridge, seminar and interview with C. L. S., Arizona State University, Tempe, Arizona, March 14, 1974.

3. "Brother Burro," text by George W. Harvey and Charles Fletcher Lummis, pictures assembled by Heather Hatch and Donald B. Sayner, *Journal of Arizona History,* vol. 17 (Winter, 1976), pp. 397-414; Donald B. Sayner and Heather Hatch, "Birdmen and Flying Machines: A Visual

Essay on Early Aviation in Arizona," *Journal of Arizona History,* vol. 15 (Winter, 1974), pp. 349-72; "The Bicycle Era in Arizona," compiled by Heather S. Hatch, *Journal of Arizona History,* vol. 13 (Spring, 1972), pp. 33-52; "Water for Phoenix: Building the Roosevelt Dam," compiled by the editors, *Journal of Arizona History,* vol. 18 (Autumn, 1977), pp. 279-94; Robert L. Spude, "Swansea, Arizona," *Journal of Arizona History,* vol. 17 (Winter, 1976), pp. 375-96; Lori Davisson, "Fifty Years at Fort Apache," *Journal of Arizona History,* vol. 17 (Autumn, 1976), pp. 301-20.

4. The man was Lieutenant John A. (Tony) Rucker, who drowned in the White River in the Chiricahua Mountains on July 11, 1878. Camp Rucker was named for him, as was Rucker Canyon in the Chiricahuas.

5. Walt Whitman, "A Noiseless, Patient Spider," in *Leaves of Grass,* ed. John Kouwenhoven, p. 351.

6. James W. Byrkix, "The IWW in Wartime Arizona," *Journal of Arizona History,* vol. 18 (Summer, 1977), pp. 149-70.

Bibliography

BOOKS AND ARTICLES

Arnold, Elliott. *Blood Brother.* New York: Duell, Sloan & Pearce, 1947.

Bandelier, Adolph A. *The Delight Makers.* New York: Dodd, Mead, 1890.

Barry, Jane. *A Time in the Sun.* Garden City, N.Y.: Doubleday, 1962.

Bergstrasser, Arnold. *Goethe's Image of Man and Society.* Chicago: Henry Regnery, 1949.

Black Elk Speaks: Being the Life Story of a Holy Man of the Oglala Sioux, as Told Through John G. Neihardt. Lincoln: University of Nebraska Press, 1969 (first publication, 1932).

Brady, Francis P. "Portrait of a Pioneer: Peter R. Brady, 1825-1902." *Journal of Arizona History,* vol. 16 (Summer, 1975), pp. 171-91.

Brown, Dee. *Bury My Heart at Wounded Knee.* New York: Bantam, 1972 (first publication, 1972).

Brown, J. Ross. *Adventures in the Apache Country: A Tour Through Arizona and Sonora.* Tucson: University of Arizona Press, 1974 (first publication, 1864).

Burroughs, Edgar Rice. *Apache Devil.* New York: Ballantine Books, 1964 (first publication, 1933).

Byrkit, James W. "The IWW in Wartime Arizona." *Journal of Arizona History,* vol. 18 (Summer, 1977), pp. 149-70.

Craig, Helen Baldock. *Within Adobe Walls.* Phoenix: Art Press Printers, 1975.

Davisson, Lori. "Fifty Years at Fort Apache." *Journal of Arizona History,* vol. 17 (Autumn, 1976), pp. 301-20.

Deloria, Vine, Jr. *God Is Red.* New York: Dell Publishing Co., 1975 (first publication, 1973).

Dickens, Charles. *Martin Chuzzlewit.* London: J. M. Dent, Everyman Series, 1967.

Edwards, M. B. "Journal." In Ralph P. Bieber. *Marching with the Army of the West.* Glendale, Calif.: Arthur H. Clark, 1936.

Emerson, Ralph Waldo. "The American Scholar." In *Nature Addresses and Lectures.* Boston: Houghton Mifflin, 1895.

———. "The Poet." In *Essays, Second Series.* Boston: Houghton Mifflin, 1895.

Faulk, Odie B. *The Arizona State Historical Society.* Tucson: Arizona Pioneers Historical Society, 1966.

Ferguson, Philip Gooch. "Diary of Philip Gooch Ferguson." In *Marching with the Army of the West,* ed. Ralph P. Bieber. Glendale, Calif.: Arthur H. Clark, 1936.

Gibson, George Rutledge. *Journal of a Soldier Under Kearny and Doniphan, 1846-1847.* Ed. Ralph P. Bieber. Glendale, Calif.: Arthur H. Clark, 1934.

Handlin, Oscar. *Truth in History.* Cambridge, Mass.: Harvard University Press, 1979.

Harvey, George, Charles Fletcher Lummis, Heather Hatch, and Donald B. Sayner. "Brother Burro." *Journal of Arizona History,* vol. 17 (Winter, 1976), pp. 397-414.

Hatch, Heather S. "The Bicycle Era in Arizona." *Journal of Arizona History,* vol. 13 (Spring, 1972), pp. 33-52.

Jacobs, Wilbur. *Dispossessing the American Indian.* New York: Scribner's, 1972.

Kane, Randy. "'An Honorable and Upright Man': Sidney R. DeLong as Post Trader at Fort Bowie." *Journal of Arizona History,* vol. 19 (Summer, 1978), pp. 297-314.

Laird, Carobeth. *Encounter with an Angry God.* Downing, Calif.: Malki Museum Press, Morongo Indian Reservation, 1975.

L'Amour, Louis. *The Lonely Men.* New York: Bantam, 1969.

Lottinville, Savoie. *The Rhetoric of History.* Norman: University of Oklahoma Press, 1976.

Luhan, Mabel Dodge. *Edge of Taos Desert.* New York: Harcourt, 1937.

Macaulay, Thomas Babington. *Critical and Historical Essays.* Arranged by A. J. Greene. London: J. M. Dent, Everyman Library, 1963.

Miller, Arthur. *Death of a Salesman.* New York: Viking, 1949.

Morley, F. V., ed. *Everybody's Boswell.* New York: Harcourt, Brace, 1930.

Nasnaga. *Indians' Summer.* New York: Holt, Rinehart & Winston, 1975.

Oswaldt, Wendell H. *This Land Was Theirs: A Study of the American Indian.* New York: John Wiley & Son, 1972 (first publication, 1966).

Pilpel, Charles. "Rehabilitation." *Harper's,* vol. 250 (January, 1975), pp. 8-9.

Pope, Alexander. "An Essay on Criticism." In *Pope's Poetical Works.* Ed. Herbert Davis. London: Oxford University Press, 1906.

Pope-Hennessey, Una. *Charles Dickens.* New York: Howell Soskin, 1946.

Radbourne, Allan. "The Naming of Mickey Free." *Journal of Arizona History*, vol. 17 (Autumn, 1976), pp. 341–46.

Ray, Joseph M. *On Becoming a University: Report on an Octennium*. El Paso: Texas Western Press, 1968.

Reeves, James. *Understanding Poetry*. London: Heinemann, 1965.

Rhodes, Eugene Manlove. *Best Novels and Short Stories*. Ed. Frank V. Dearing. Boston: Houghton Mifflin, 1949.

Rickards, Colin. *Bowler Hats and Stetsons: Stories of Englishmen in the Wild West*. London: Ronald Whiting and Wheaton, 1966.

Rosa, Joseph G. *They Called Him Wild Bill: The Life and Adventures of James Butler Hickok*. 2d ed. Norman: University of Oklahoma Press, 1974 (1st ed., 1964).

———, and Robin May. *Gunsmoke: A Study of Violence in the Wild West*. London: New English Library, 1977.

Ross, Chuck. "Rejected." *New West*, vol. 4 (February 12, 1979), pp. 34–43.

Ryan, Marah Ellis. *Indian Love Letters*. Chicago: McClurg, 1907.

Sayner, Donald B., and Heather Hatch. "Birdmen and Flying Machines: A Visual Essay on Early Aviation in Arizona." *Journal of Arizona History*, vol. 15 (Winter, 1974), pp. 349–72.

Schellie, Don. *Vast Domain of Blood*. Los Angeles: Westernlore, 1968.

Schlesinger, Arthur M., Jr. *The Age of Jackson*. Boston: Little, Brown, 1950.

Sewell, Elizabeth. *Human Metaphor*. South Bend, Ind.: University of Notre Dame Press, 1964.

Shelley, Percy Bysshe. "Shelley's Defense of Poetry." In *The Four Ages of Poetry*. Percy Reprints no. 3. Oxford: Basil Blackwell, 1921.

Sidney, Sir Philip. *The Miscellaneous Works of Sir Philip Sidney, Knt.* Ed. William Gray. Boston: T. O. P. H. Burnham, 1860.

———. *Sidney's Apologie for Poetry*. Ed. J. Churton Collins. Oxford: Clarendon Press, 1907.

Smith, Cornelius C., Jr. *William Sanders Oury: History Maker of the Southwest*. Tucson: University of Arizona Press, 1967.

Smithwick, Noah. *The Evolution of a State; or Recollections of Old Texas Days*. Austin, Texas: Steck-Vaughn, 1968 (first publication, 1900).

Sonnichsen, C. L. "The Ambivalent Apache." *Western American Literature*, vol. 10 (August, 1975), pp. 99–114.

———. *The El Paso Salt War*. El Paso: Texas Western Press, 1961.

———. "Jonathan Gillam and the White Man's Burden." *Persimmon Hill,*vol. 6 (Winter, 1974), pp. 52-57.

———. "Jonathan Gillam and the White Man's Burden." In Western Writers of America. *Spurs.* New York: Bantam, 1977, pp. 456-68.

———. *The Mescalero Apaches.* Norman: University of Oklahoma Press, 1972 (first publication, 1958).

———. *Pass of the North: Four Centuries on the Río Grande.* El Paso: Texas Western Press, 1968.

Spude, Robert L. "Swansea, Arizona." *Journal of Arizona History,* vol. 17 (Winter, 1976), pp. 375-96.

Stearns, Peter, and Joel A. Tarr. "Born Again Historians Stepping out of Academic Closet." *Arizona Daily Star,* June 17, 1980.

Stegner, Wallace. *The Uneasy Chair: A Biography of Bernard De Voto.* Garden City, N.Y.: Doubleday & Co., 1974.

Steinbeck, John. "The Leader of the People." In *The Golden Argosy: A Collection of the Most Celebrated Stories in the English Language,* ed. Van H. Cartmell and Charles Grayson. New York: Dial, 1964.

Steiner, Stan. *The Vanishing White Man.* New York: Harper & Row, 1977 (first publication, 1976).

Terrell, John Upton. *Apache Chronicle.* New York: World, 1972.

Tolkien, J. R. R. *Beowulf, the Monsters and the Critics.* Sir Israel Gollancz Memorial Lectures, British Academy, 1936. London: H. Milford, [1936].

Turner, Ronny E., and Charles K. Edgley. "'The Devil Made Me Do It!' Popular Culture and Religious Vocabularies of Motive." *Journal of Popular Culture,* vol. 8 (Summer, 1974), pp. 28-34.

"Water for Phoenix: Building the Roosevelt Dam." *Journal of Arizona History,* vol. 18 (Autumn, 1977), pp. 279-94.

Webb, Walter Prescott. *The Great Frontier.* Austin: University of Texas Press, 1964.

Western Writers of America. *Spurs.* New York: Bantam, 1977.

Whitman, Walt. "A Noiseless, Patient Spider." In *Leaves of Grass,* ed. John Kouwenhoven. New York: Modern Library, 1950.

Wiley, Bell Irvin. *The Life of Johnny Reb, the Common Soldier of the Confederacy.* Indianapolis, Ind.: Bobbs-Merrill, 1943.

Wolfe, Thomas. *The Face of a Nation: Poetical Passages from the Writings of Thomas Wolfe.* New York: Literary Guild of America, [1939].

Wordsworth, William. "Ode on the Intimations of Immortality." In *Oxford Anthology of English Poetry*, ed. Howard Foster Lowry. New York: Oxford University Press, 1956.

Wright, Harold Bell. *The Mine with the Iron Door*. New York: Appleton, 1923.

MANUSCRIPTS AND DOCUMENTS

Alcazar Book Service, El Paso, Texas. Catalogue 156, Winter–Spring, 1978–79.

Arizona Pioneers Historical Society Register, 1888–1895. Arizona Historical Society.

Arpad, Joseph. "The Relations of Folklore and Popular Culture Studies." MS. Paper read at the 1975 meeting of the American Folklore Society. Copy provided by Arpad.

Condition of the Indian Tribes: Report of the Joint Special Committee Appointed Under the Joint Resolution of March 3, 1865. Washington, D.C.: Government Printing Office, 1867.

Farris, Frances Bramlette, and C. L. Sonnichsen. "South of the Alamo." MS.

Olney, Austin G. Letter to *Time*, vol. 113 (March 19, 1979), pp. 7–8.

Oury, William Sanders. "The Camp Grant Massacre." Paper read before the Arizona Pioneers Historical Society, April 6, 1885. Typescript, W. S. Oury file, Arizona Historical Society, Tucson.

———. Speech Made at the Completion of the S.P.R.R., Tucson, March 20, 1880. Copy in W. S. Oury file, Arizona Historical Society, Tucson.

INTERVIEWS

Farrington Carpenter, Hayden, Colorado, April 28, 1949.

Tom Cannon, El Paso, Texas, February 26, 1976.

Martin Ridge, Tempe, Arizona, March 14, 1979.

Winter Griffith, Tucson, Arizona, January 4, 1980.

Acknowledgments

For permission to reprint the following selections I am grateful:

"The Poetry of History," *The American West* 12, no. 5 (September, 1975): 26-27, 59-60. © 1975 by The American West Publishing Company, Cupertino, California. Reprinted by permission of the publisher.

"The Ambidextrous Historian" (originally "The Poor Wayfaring Scholar"), *The Journal of Popular Culture* 10, no. 1 (Summer, 1976):88-95.

"John Doe, O. H. M." (originally "Toward an Order of Minor Historians"), *The American West* 11, no. 2 (March, 1974):48, 62-63. © 1974 by The American West Publishing Company, Cupertino, California. Reprinted by permission of the publisher.

"Dracula in the Stacks," *Wilson Library Bulletin* 51, no. 5 (January, 1977): 419-23.

"The Fine Art of Plagiarism" (originally "The Folklore of Academe"), *Nova* 8, no. 3 (June, 1973):3-5.

Index